Fortissimi and Validissimi

The Batavian Auxiliaries of the Roman army

Rada Varga

Helion & Company Limited
Unit 8 Amherst Business Centre
Budbrooke Road
Warwick
CV34 5WE
England
Tel. 01926 499 619
Email: info@helion.co.uk
Website: www.helion.co.uk
X, formerly Twitter: @helionbooks
Visit our blog https://helionbooks.wordpress.com/

Published by Helion & Company 2025
Designed and typeset by Mary Woolley, Battlefield Design (www.battlefield-design.co.uk)
Cover designed by Paul Hewitt, Battlefield Design (www.battlefield-design.co.uk)

Text © Rada Varga 2025
Photographs and illustrations © as individually credited
Cover artworks by Giorgio Albertini © Helion & Company 2025
Maps by Anderson Subtil © Helion & Company 2025

Every reasonable effort has been made to trace copyright holders and to obtain their permission for the use of copyright material. The author and publisher apologise for any errors or omissions in this work and would be grateful if notified of any corrections that should be incorporated in future reprints or editions of this book.

ISBN 978-1-804518-26-7

British Library Cataloguing-in-Publication Data.
A catalogue record for this book is available from the British Library.

All rights reserved. No part of this publication may be reproduced, stored in a retrieval system, or transmitted, in any form, or by any means, electronic, mechanical, photocopying, recording or otherwise, without the express written consent of Helion & Company Limited.

For details of other military history titles published by Helion & Company Limited contact the above address or visit our website: http://www.helion.co.uk.

We always welcome receiving book proposals from prospective authors.

Contents

Introduction v

1 The Emergence of the Batavians in the Low Rhine Region ... 7
2 Historical Turning Point: The Batavian Rebellion 25
  Chronology of the Rebellion 47
3 The Batavians in the Roman Fold 49
4 Military Equipment and Fighting Technique 78
5 The Batavians Rediscovered 88

Appendices:
I   Glossary 93
II   Roman Monetary System 95
III List of Roman Emperors 96
IV   Short Biographiess of the Ancient Authors Mentioned In The Book 98

Bibliographical Essay and Bibliography 101

Introduction

This book delves into the history of the Batavians, a Germanic tribe who served as auxiliary soldiers for the Roman Empire during the Principate. Their history is known through literary sources, epigraphy, and archaeological discoveries. In this work, the author has attempted to distil the essence of the various types of information into a coherent narrative, including the Batavians' identity within and beyond the borders of their native Lower Rhine region.

In the following chapters, we will mark the major milestones of Batavian history, such as the emergence of the tribe during the Iron Age and its identity constructs, the Batavian rebellion that almost broke them from the Roman imperial fold, and the history of the Batavian homeland and troops abroad during the second and third centuries. The final two smaller chapters focus on the military equipment and fighting style of the Batavians, as well as their rediscovery and reception in modern times. As the target audience for this book is broad, we have included a brief bibliographic essay in addition to the reference list. Additionally, annexes such as a glossary, chronological list of emperors, description of the Roman monetary system, and biographical medallions of the ancient authors mentioned in the book are included.

The Lower Rhine region was a border territory during Roman times, and the frequent displacement of troops ensured that soldiers had a significant influence on the cultural transformation processes that occurred in this area. The *Batavi* initially consisted of ethnic soldiers who had a treaty with Rome. They oversaw the supply of men to the Roman auxiliary units, led by their native aristocracy. The Batavian soldiers were known for their loyalty and ferocity, which earned them a place as elite soldiers and personal guards of the emperors.

Regardless (as well as due to) their extraordinary status, in 69 AD they were the protagonists of one of the fiercest rebellions faced by the Roman Empire during the first century. Led by a Romanized aristocrat, named Julius Civilis, they defied and challenged Rome's rule over the Lower Rhine territories. Historians have access to a relatively high quantity of information about the rebellion, including literary descriptions and archaeological findings, allowing for a more comprehensive understanding of the events. In the spring of 70 AD, after posing a significant threat to the

Empire, Civilis engaged in peace talks and the Batavians were reintegrated into the Roman fold.

After the revolt, the Batavian troops were reorganised, but apparently still led by their own aristocracy (this was a topic subjected to historiographic debate, detailed herewithin). The cohorts were moved to Britannia, being part in the famous battle of Mons Graupius, where the Roman troops, led by Agricola, faced the Caledonians. The Batavian troops performed exceptionally well, living up to their reputation. One of the Batavian cohorts was stationed at Vindolanda, the famous fort where numerous wax tablets were discovered. These tablets contain private documents, such as lists and letters, which offer glimpses into day to day military life. In one of them, written by the *decurio* Masclus, the prefect Flavius Cerialis is refered to as *rex*, providing insight into Batavian ethnic culture and tradition. Cerialis, a figure who will be discussed further in the book, appears to have descended from the former tribal royalty, like Civilis before him, but keeping to his vow of loyalty to Rome.

In contrast to other European populations and tribes that were integrated into the Roman Empire, the Batavians have a well-documented post-conquest history, at least up to a certain point. Our knowledge of them is not limited to written sources, as they are also revealed through archaeological finds. As a result, we have gained an insight into their military equipment and a material culture consistent with that of a frontier people. In the provinces where various Batavian troops were stationed, such as Pannonia and Dacia, there are imports from the Rhine as well as locally specific objects. These bear witness to the preservation of their Germanic roots concurrent to their integration into a new society.

As an archaeologist, I have a personal interest in this extraordinary people and in bringing their story to a wider audience, as I am part of the coordinating team of the excavations carried on site where the Batavian elite cavalry troop was stationed in Roman Dacia, for more than 100 years (at Războieni-Cetate, in Romania). As for this, the chapter on the *ala* benefits from new research, which make whole the story of the Batavians in later ages, during the mid-third century.

In this context, it is worth noting that this book is the result of years of archaeological excavations and research into the history and material culture of the Batavians. It is impossible to mention all the individuals and outlets that have contributed to its making, but I am forever grateful for their assistance. I must mention a fellowship granted by the Gerda Henkel Foundation and a project financed by the Romanian Ministry of Research and Innovation. Both were fundamental in advancing and developing my research. Also, I must express my thanks to my colleagues with whom I share the archaeological excavation site from Războieni.

Finally, the story of the Batavians is still being written. Archaeology and new interdisciplinary methods continue to bring forth new data and open up possibilities for new interpretations. This book is dedicated to all those curious about discovering an ancient, yet perhaps not so distant past.

1

The Emergence of the Batavians in the Low Rhine Region

Who were the Batavians?

The Batavians were a prominent Germanic population of Antiquity, whose history was and remains of great interest to historians, archaeologists and the general public. They were quickly integrated into the Roman Empire and identified themselves as elite warriors, particularly cavalrymen, of the Imperial army. In recent times, they even became part of the popular culture in certain areas of Europe due to their appealing stories, renowned military skills and interesting material culture.

However, their origins and emergence into European written history remain unclear. The earliest written sources about them come from Roman writers, as is the case with other 'barbarian' populations from central and northern Europe. Julius Caesar does not mention the Batavians as a tribe in his *Commentarii de Bello Gallico*. However, he does refer to an 'island of the Batavians' – *insula Batavorum* – in the Rhine. This 'island' (which was actually a patch of land, not a real island) was a fertile, albeit small, region formed by the Low Rhine and the Waal river.

According to Tacitus,[1] the Batavians originated from a branch of the *Chatti*, but this information, however plausible, remains speculative. In his storyline, the *Chatti* migrated from their homeland due to internal conflicts and settled on an 'island' that was supposedly uninhabited at the time. And while the former claim is disputed, the latter is entirely false and contradicted by archaeological evidence, which shows continuous habitation in the Batavian homeland area since the Iron Age into Roman times.

---

1   Tacitus, *Germania* I 29.

Caesar's wars and the birth of the Batavian ethos

The true story, as reconstructed from both literary and archaeological sources, is complex and tragic. Despite Caesar's reputation as a great reformer, talented political and military leader, and overall decent human being in the context of his time and its tribulations, his conquest of Gaul was marred by numerous brutal episodes.

During the Late Iron Age, just prior to Caesar's conquest, the *Eburones*, a powerful Gaulish tribe, occupied the territory between the Ardennes and the Rhine-Maas delta. The tribe was led by two kings[2] and had a typically tribal, rather lax organisation. Initially, they were important allies for Caesar in the area. Nico Roymans, a renowned researcher of Batavian identity, has suggested, based on archaeological findings and deductive reasoning, that the *Eburones* inhabited the eastern part of the Delta, specifically the subsequent Batavian territory.[3] By all data we nowadays have, this assumption seems to be correct.

It is challenging to provide a detailed account of the periods preceding constant contact with the Romans due to the lack of written sources. During the Late Iron Age, elite groups of horsemen known as the *comitatus* emerged, serving tribal leaders and becoming the core of social institutions and traditions. This feature, skilled cavalrymen, would later define Batavian identity. The mounted warriors were also present in the Lower Rhine region, which would eventually become Batavian territory, during Caesar's conquest when they were part of the *Eburones*. The impression they left on Caesar was significant, as evidenced by his subsequent establishment of a personal guard consisting of 400 Germanic cavalrymen. This group is considered to be the forerunner of the Flavian imperial guard, which was primarily composed of Batavians. Archaeologically pinpointing the existence of the *comitatus* is difficult, but the consistent presence of horse bones and long swords from the period[4] strongly corroborate the literary sources.

During the 'classical' Batavian period, commerce remained regional, with most contacts established with the northern Gaulish and Middle Rhine regions. However, there was an addition of contacts with the Mediterranean and imports of luxury goods from the Roman Empire. These factors impacted significantly on society, its elites, their political views, and their understanding of their place within the Empire.

The Batavian tribe based its functioning on the regional Late Iron Age realities. However, the most significant factor that led to their emergence in history was Caesar's conquest of Gaul and its consequences for Western

---

2   Caesar, *De bello Gallico* VI 31.5.
3   N. Roymans, *Ethnic identity and imperial power. The Batavians in the early Roman Empire* (Amsterdam: Amsterdam University Press, 2004), p. 23.
4   Roymans, *Ethnic identity*, p. 20.

Europe. The conquest resulted in mass enslavement, plundering, and genocide, which led to migrations, ethnic shuffling, and significant changes in the identity paradigms of various tribes.

The fate of the *Eburones* is linked to the settlement of the Batavians in their traditional territory during the classical era. In 54 BC, the *Eburones*, who were previously allies of Caesar, rebelled and defeated a Roman legion. However, the aftermath was tragic for the tribe as they were brutally retaliated against by the Romans, causing them to disappear from history and the political map. The objective of this process was not complete physical annihilation, but rather the dismantling of the tribal organisation, elimination of the elites and warrior groups, and integration of the remaining population into other groups.

Between Caesar's departure for Rome in 51 BC and Drusus' arrival in Germania in 15 BC, several populations were relocated with Roman assistance from the east of the Rhine to its western shore. The *Batavi* were also relocated during this time. The *Ubii*, for example, moved entirely to the west of the Rhine, settling in the Cologne area. The *Tungri*, who were identified by Tacitus as descendants of the first groups of Germans to cross the Rhine, occupied parts of the Belgic region at the beginning of the imperial era.[5] As previously mentioned, the *Batavi* also migrated during this period, as a branch of the *Chatti* who came from the Middle Rhine area and settled in the Rhine/Maas delta. It is likely that the core of this population consisted of a tribal warrior leader and his followers, who were urged and aided by Rome to relocate to this area. All of these tribes occupied territories that were previously controlled by the Eburonean coalition. Therefore, a connection can be made between the extinction of the *Eburones* and these migration movements. Rome was behind these population shifts and political dynamics, but other factors may have also played a role, such as internal conflicts, demographic overgrowth, and pressure from other tribes.

Although the main stages of the migration story can be delineated today, the matter remains complicated. Historians are cautious whenever ancient literature mentions people settling into 'empty places'. Almost always it is an exaggeration and the newly migrated groups mixed with remnants of the local population. Archaeology may shed light on this, but it is difficult in our case as we are dealing with tribes that have very similar material culture and have had commercial contacts in the past. Additionally, we are trying to distinguish changes that occurred over a short period of time, making it difficult to discern archaeological differences. Despite the challenges of identifying archaeological evidence, it can be concluded that there was no significant interruption in habitation in the Batavian region identifiable through archaeological means, nor was there evidence of widespread destruction. However, a decline in population and habitation during the 1st century BC is archaeologically identifiable, indicating that Caesar's

---

5   Tacitus, *Germania* II 5.

FORTISSIMI AND VALIDISSIMI: THE BATAVIAN AUXILIARIES OF THE ROMAN ARMY

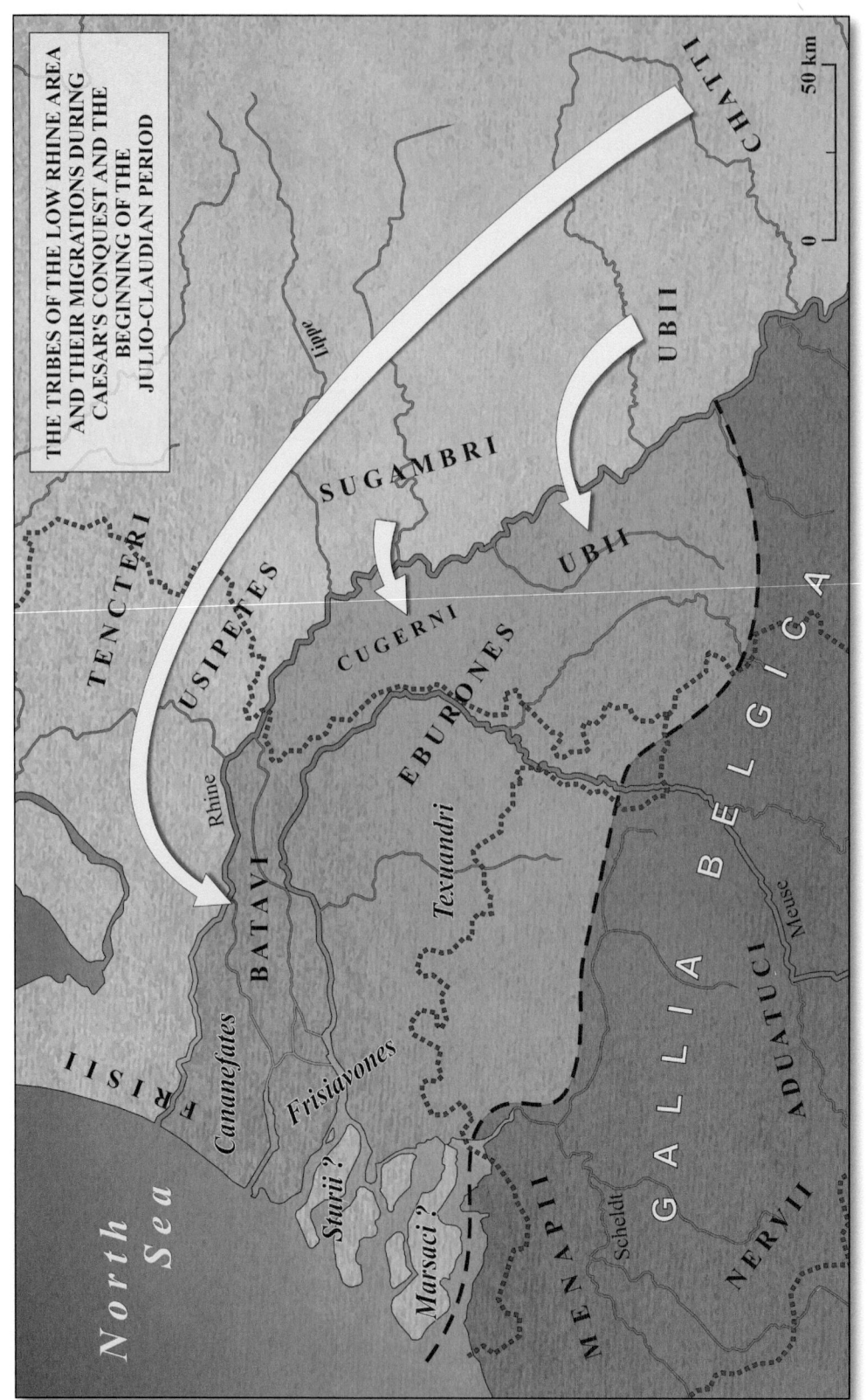

The tribes of the Low Rhine area and their migrations during Caesar's conquest and the beginning of the Julio-Claudian period.

campaigns had both quantitative and qualitative impacts on the local populations. Therefore, it is likely that an elite group, possibly from the *Chatti* tribe as indicated by Tacitus, merged with the remaining members of the local population, including the *Eburones* and their allies. This process contributed to the formation of Batavian identity and culture.

The Julio-Claudian period and the beginning of recorded history

Batavian history is divided by modern historiography into two major periods: pre-revolt and post-revolt. The first stages of Batavian history are relatively well known, dating back to the Julio-Claudians. Following Nero's death, the Batavians rebelled and entered a new stage of their existence during the Flavian period, which continued throughout the Principate.

According to Tacitus,[6] the Batavians had a treaty with Rome since Julio-Claudian times. They provided men to the Roman auxiliary units, led by their native aristocracy, and were exempted from paying tribute in exchange. In 12 BC, Drusus, Augustus' stepson and one of the most prominent military leaders of the time, used the Batavian territory as a basecamp for his campaigns into Germania Magna.

Drusus' relationship with the Batavi is a well-established fact and a significant milestone. However, it is possible that their relationship with the Roman power dates back even earlier, as mentioned a few pages ago. While the references are scarce and inconclusive, they should not be disregarded. Caesar himself mentions fighting alongside Germanic auxiliaries during the civil war and in Egypt.[7] It is unclear what 'Germanic' meant to him and where they primarily originated from, but two episodes stand out in particular. In these episodes, Caesar sent his auxiliaries to cross rivers in full armour, in one instance to swim the Nile and find fords where his army could cross the river. Historians have drawn comparisons to the Batavians, who later became known for their ability to cross rivers in almost any conditions while fully geared. However, it is uncertain whether the Batavian identity was established during this period or if they still identified as *Chatti* at the time. Lucanus makes another reference to Caesar's Germanic forces in Pharsalia, specifically and explicitly mentioning his Batavian auxiliaries.[8] The term has been criticised as an anachronism, likely added by a later copyist. However, it is possible that Caesar did have Germanic troops from the area that would later be inhabited by the Batavians and use of this term by the copyist is therefore understandable and just. Although it is uncertain whether Caesar himself referred to them as *Batavi*, it is likely that they originated from the same region and were the precursors of the future Batavian cavalry.

---

6   Tacitus, *Germania* XXIX 1; *Historiae* IV 12.
7   Caesar, *De bello civili* I 83.5; *De bello Alexandrino* XXIX 2.
8   Lucanus, *Pharsalia* I 431.

FORTISSIMI AND VALIDISSIMI: THE BATAVIAN AUXILIARIES OF THE ROMAN ARMY

It can be confirmed that Caesar's primary allies in the Middle Rhine were the *Ubii*, who were freed from the *Suebi* of Ariovistus, and the *Chatti*, who may have been in a similar situation. As part of the agreement with Rome, a faction of the *Chatti* settled in the Rhine/Maas Delta and merged with the local population, forming the community later known as the Batavi. It is unclear whether the name existed prior to this resettlement or emerged during this period.

Archaeologically, there is evidence supporting the placement of the early stages of the treaty with Rome during Caesar's time. This evidence includes military attire parts, such as a helmet, as well as hoards comprising Roman denarii along local coins.[9] However, there are no accounts of who led the migration during this period. Later clues suggest that the Batavians had some form of royalty at one point. According to Tacitus, Julius Civilis, the leader of the Batavian rebellion in 69 AD, was *regia stirpe*[10] and later on, a decurio from Vindolanda mesmerisingly addresses his commander with the appellative *rex*.[11] This suggests that some members of the tribal aristocracy held a right to lead above others. However, during the Principate, royalty did not seem to function as such, as there is no evidence of a client king among the Batavians. It is likely that the Batavian Julii obtained citizenship at the start of the tribe's alliance with Rome and were part of the royal family/families and the first generation of high aristocracy. While some members of the tribe may have been granted citizenship as a reward for their service to the emperors, the aristocracy, particularly the families regarded as royalty and leaders during the settlement period, were granted citizenship through the initial treaty, which established a direct relationship with the Julian emperors.

During the Roman period, the royal institution was replaced by a Roman-style magistrate. An inscription from Ruimel, dated in the first half of the 1st century AD, provides some clues. It records a certain Flavus as the *summus magistratus* of the *civitas Batavorum*.[12] Although the title is not typical and is not attested elsewhere, it appears that only one person held the position, indicating that the Roman principle of collegiality was not respected in this case. Despite the lack of other attestations, this is not an aberration. Similar situations occurred in the Gallic *civitates* during the first decades of their integration into the Empire. The magistrate was likely elected by a remnant of the tribal council. Although not necessarily part of the royalty, he was probably a member of the tribal aristocracy, who produced the elite warriors and commanded the general respect of the community.

---

9   Roymans, *Ethnic identity*, p. 60.
10 Tacitus, *Historiae* IV 13 and IV 32.
11 *Tabulae Vindolandenses* III 628.
12 CIL XIII 8771.

Imperial guards and the emergence of the Batavian identity construct

It has been previously established that the Batavians settled in their historical territory and formed a military relationship with Rome during Caesar's era, although this period is not fully documented. But it was during the Julio-Claudian period that the Batavians became Rome's most formidable auxiliaries.

Subsequently, they served as traditional guards for the Roman emperor. This traditional bodyguard corps may have originated from Caesar's personal guards' corps, as mentioned. The reason for selecting Germanic bodyguards was due to their military skills and apparent loyalty, as well as playing into the Roman stereotype of fearless Germanic warriors, which was intimidating even before they had to prove their prowess. It is worth noting that King Herod the Great of Judea was so impressed by Augustus' Germanic guards that he modelled a unit of Germanic bodyguards for himself.[13] It is reasonable to assume that the Batavian units had a significant impact on many onlookers, making them ideal as imperial guards. The Julio-Claudian imperial guard was at one point colloquially referred to as the *Batavi*,[14] due to its Batavian core (and also possibly due to a certain degree of ethnic generalisation made by the Romans), while it was officially known as the *Germani corporis custodes*. In some cases, when the guards died young during service, their tribal appurtenance was mentioned on the tombstones erected for them in Rome. The funerals of *Batavi, Ubi, Tungri*, were conducted by a *collegium Germanorum*,[15] which was an association of soldiers organised according to the typical Roman associative model.

The tombstones of the early cavalry guards reveal their Batavian origin in many cases, as well as their names. Decoding onomastics, the question of what a name truly says about the ethnic identity and origins of the bearer must always be on the historian's mind. It is important to consider whether a name is the result of trends or whims, a reflection of the family's culture or immediate entourage, rather than objective factors. There is no universal answer to this issue as each situation has its own unique characteristics. The tombstones from Rome reveal that Latin and Greek names have been a common feature of Batavian onomastics over the years. Greek names were adopted by Batavian military families after northern recruits from the Flavian Imperial Guard introduced them, possibly to replace Batavian/Germanic names unpronounceable for the inhabitants of the capital.[16]

---

13 M.P. Speidel, *Riding for Caesar* (London, New York: Routledge, 1994), pp. 12–18; S. Rocca, *The Army of Herod the Great* (Oxford: Osprey Publishing, 2009): pp. 15–16. Herod's Germanic guards were an important presence at the king's funeral (Josephus, *Jewish War* I 671–673).
14 Suetonius, *Caligula* 43; Cassius Dio, *Historiae Romanae* LV 24.
15 AE 1952, 145–149; AE 1968, 32.
16 A. Birley, 'The names of the Batavians and Tungrians', in T. Grünewald (ed.),

However, they later became a symbol of military families' tradition. General Batavian onomastics, widespread throughout Europe up to the 3rd century AD, are characterised by the use of Latin names and the absence of Germanic names.

The Roman recruitment system

In addition to the imperial guard, which consisted of approximately 500 men, regular auxiliary troops were also recruited during the Julio-Claudian period. This indicates a strong military tradition within the entire tribe, rather than exclusively among the aristocracy. Prior to the rebellion, there was one *ala* and eight cohorts,[17] totalling 5,000 men in theory. These troops were recruited, at least initially, from the Batavian group. The actual number of men was lower, but a figure around 4,000 would still be a significant amount. Recruitment and the Batavian auxiliaries functioning within the Roman army were successful due to physical qualities, traditional skills, and a tightly knit social structure that ensured loyalty to local leaders. However, loyalty to Rome was the most crucial aspect of this structure. The Batavian prefects, commanders of the troops, where part of the highest networks of the area, and due to client relationships, probably had and maintained a personal relationship with Drusus, Tiberius, Germanicus.[18]

The Batavians' reputation as a reliable source of soldiers is also to be linked with the unique characteristics of their homeland. Although the region is fertile, it is limited in size and grazing opportunities are restricted by seasonal flooding.[19] The Batavians did not pay taxes to Rome, but it is likely that parts of the population were obligated to provide levies to local leaders as well. Therefore, the recruitment policy and provision of men for the army was the only means for the Batavians to physically subsist in their territory. Ironically, these conditions necessitated small-scale agricultural activities and led to family self-sufficiency. Household production in Germanic societies was typically managed by women, leading Caesar and

---

Germania inferior. Besiedllung, Gesellschaft und Wirtschaft an der Grenze der römisch-germanischen Welt, RGA Ergänzungsband 28 (Berlin, New York: de Gruyter, 2001); T. Derks, 'Ethnic identity in the Roman frontier. The epigraphy of Batavi and other Lower Rhine tribes', in T. Derks, N. Roymans (eds.), *Ethnic Constructs in Antiquity. The role of power and tradition* (Amsterdam: Amsterdam University Press, 2009), pp. 239–282; C. van Driel-Murray, 'Ethnic Soldiers: The Experience of the Lower Rhine Tribes', in T. Grunewald, S. Seibel (eds.), *Kontinuitat und Diskontinuitat* (Berlin: de Gruyter, 2003), pp. 200–217.

17   These were the typically auxiliary forces of the Roman army. The *alae* were cavalry units, while the *cohortes* were pedestrian troops.
18   J. Slofstra, 'Batavians and Romans on the Lower Rhine', *Archaeological Dialogues*, 9, 2002, p. 29.
19   L.I. Kooistra, *Borderland Farming. Possibilities and limitations of farming in the Roman period and early Middle Ages between Rhine and Meuse* (Assen/Amersfoort: Van Gorcum/Rijksdienst voor Oudheidkundig Bodemonderzoek, 1996).

Tacitus to observe that men were often idle and lazy according to Roman standards. This was likely due to the fact that the household was structured around the work of women and children, a state of facts which was generally not uncommon in traditional societies.

Recruits for the Batavian troops were drawn from all social layers, but the demographic pool of the tribe alone could not have sustained them long-term. Worth mentioning that the Batavians also joined other troops, as it is suggested by inscriptions of Batavian soldiers serving in other Roman auxiliary troops. One of them is a certain Imerix from Burnum (in Croatia), who was a Batavian and served in the ala Hispanorum, sometimes between 9–41 AD.[20] Archaeological evidence does not support the existence of a 'true' aristocracy, with extravagant houses and goods, but rather suggests an egalitarian society. Considering the relatively poor economic conditions of the area, it is likely that the money earned from military service was primarily used for minor household expenses and non-archaeologically identifiable goods such as textiles, food, livestock.[21] The abundance of *fibulae* found in certain rural settlements suggests that these items were even popular gifts and had a social function, indicating status.

The Roman military service and recruitment had both positive and negative effects on the Batavian community. On the one hand, it provided a constant income that was necessary for the whole tribe. On the other hand, it also took a demographic toll. Despite these advantages and disadvantages, the integration of the Batavian community within the Roman army gave them a certain status, helped build their identity, and most likely instilled a sense of pride.

Noviomagus and its hinterland

Noviomagus served as the historical capital of the Batavians, and its evolution is closely tied to the transgressions of the tribe. However, to fully comprehend the development and changes undergone by the settlement, it is essential to consider the movements of the Empire in the region, specifically Augustus' and Tiberius' campaigns in the Rhine area.

Following his victory in the civil war at Actium (31 BC), Augustus directed his attention and resources towards the complete integration and assimilation of the north and western provinces. His effort resulted in a fierce war against the *Cantabri*, during which Augustus nearly lost his life due to illness. However, resources were also allocated to the Rhine area during this time. The first Roman emperor aimed to conquer Germania up to the river Elbe. However, this was likely not a well-defined plan from the outset, but rather a strategy influenced by various factors, ambitions, and factual developments.

---

20 N. Cesarik, 'The inscription of a Batavian horseman from the Archaeological Museum Zadar', *Zeitschrift für Papyrologie und Epigraphik*, 199, 2016, pp. 234–236.
21 van Driel-Murray, *Ethnic Soldiers*, p. 208.

FORTISSIMI AND VALIDISSIMI: THE BATAVIAN AUXILIARIES OF THE ROMAN ARMY

It is possible that Augustus became personally interested in and felt the need to intervene in the Rhine area after the *clades Lolliana* in 16 BC, when the governor Marcus Lollius was defeated by a coalition of Germanic tribes and lost a legionary eagle.[22] In response to the Empire's military shame, Augustus sent his stepson Drusus to the Rhine. The joint successes of Drusus and his brother Tiberius in Rhaetia and the Alps were generally considered a triumph, but the situation in Germania still had to be stabilised. Drusus likely oversaw the construction of several military forts in the area during his campaigns from 12–9 BC. This was the first time the strength of the Batavian alliance was tested in local wars against other Germanic tribes. Drusus reached the Elbe River in the area of modern-day Dresden or Magdeburg and decided to halt his advance. According to legend, Drusus saw the apparition of a woman, presumably Germania, warning him not to proceed. However, as a skilled tactician and experienced commander, he must have known that maintaining the logistics chain and supply income would have been nearly impossible once he crossed the river. On his return from the Elbe, he fell off his horse and injured his leg. Although the initial wound appeared to be minor, it became infected and he died within a month. Following this tragedy, Tiberius assumed command of the Rhine army and organised Drusus' conquests, resulting in Germania becoming a regular province. However, disaster struck again in the year 9 when Publius Quinctilius Varus, who was not the governor of Gaul like his predecessors in the area, but of the newly established Germania, was defeated at the Teutoburg Forest, resulting in the destruction of three legions and many auxiliary troops. The defeat had a devastating impact on the province, and the border was pushed back to the Rhine. As a consequence, Rome established a permanent frontier along this river.

Following the death of Augustus in 14, the responsibility of managing Germania and the Germanic tribes fell to his successor, Tiberius. Being familiar with the situation in the region, the new emperor dispatched Germanicus, the son of the late Drusus, to restore order in Germania. But in 16, Tiberius recalled him due to his lack of success, his

The bronze statue of Germanicus from Museo Archaeologico di Amelia. It is a later statue, probably commissioned by Germanicus' brother, Claudius, after he was proclaimed emperor

---

22 Tacitus, *Annales* I 10 and III 48. As a side note, this Lollius was a shady character who in some ways mirrored the future vain or incompetent generals who would face the tribes of the Rhine. In later years, after leaving Gaul, he was Caius Caesar's tutor, and the latter denounced him for accepting bribes from the Parthian king. To avoid punishment, Lollius committed suicide, leaving behind a vast fortune amassed during his governorships of various provinces.

only real accomplishment being the retrieving of the eagles lost by Varus. Tacitus and Suetonius both portrayed Tiberius in a negative light, citing his jealousy towards his young nephew. However, avoiding any subjective evaluations, it is a fact that Germanicus' army was a burden on the Gaulish provinces, his advancements were minimal, and his retrieval of the eagles likely marked the end of Rome's aspirations for a province north and east of the Rhine. It is important to note that any personal reasons for Tiberius' actions should not be completely disregarded, but they should not be the sole focus of the discussion. The area west of the Rhine became part of Gallia Belgica on paper, but real authority belonged to the commanders of the Germanic armies. One must also state that Lower and Upper Germania were founded only later, during the 80s; the Julio-Claudians somehow couldn't fully face and put into law the reality of the Germanic failure. Their most celebrated generals, the most popular 'princes' of their house, won their renown in Germania and telling the world, officially, that all they had done had been for nothing was distressful.

***

The Batavians' home area was discussed from an agricultural and economic perspective. However, it was also strategically suited. From the south, it was the last high and dry location south of the Rhine and the convergence point of routes along the Rhine and Maas, including the future roads to Tongres and Cologne.

The heart of the Batavian territory and administration was in modern-day Nijmegen, known as Roman Noviomagus. At the start of their history, the location was known as *oppidum Batavorum* (or Batavodurum). Many questions still remain regarding its institutions and civil administration. The *oppidum* had the urbanistic structure of a *vicus*, which was a Roman-style, orderly (quasi-)rural settlement covering approximately 20 hectares. It was surrounded by a ditch, although there are indications that this was only constructed during the rebellion in 69–70 AD.

The oppidum had a Roman style planimetry from the start, as it was built as a capital city. However, it is unclear whether it was built as the capital 'of' or 'for' the Batavians.

During Drusus' campaign, a large legionary camp was built on the location called Hunerberg, which hosted around 15,000 soldiers. After Drusus' death, the fort was dismantled. Another military installation had also existed on the Kops-Plateau, to the east, since around 12 BC. The structure was smaller in size and adapted to its position on the highest promontory in the area, taking on a triangular shape.

The relationship between the civilian and military settlements was one of cohabitation, with the *vicus* not being an extension of the military fort. Interestingly, during this early stage of their history, the oppidum from Valkhof and the Kops Plateau were separated by a cemetery, in which around 1,500

FORTISSIMI AND VALIDISSIMI: THE BATAVIAN AUXILIARIES OF THE ROMAN ARMY

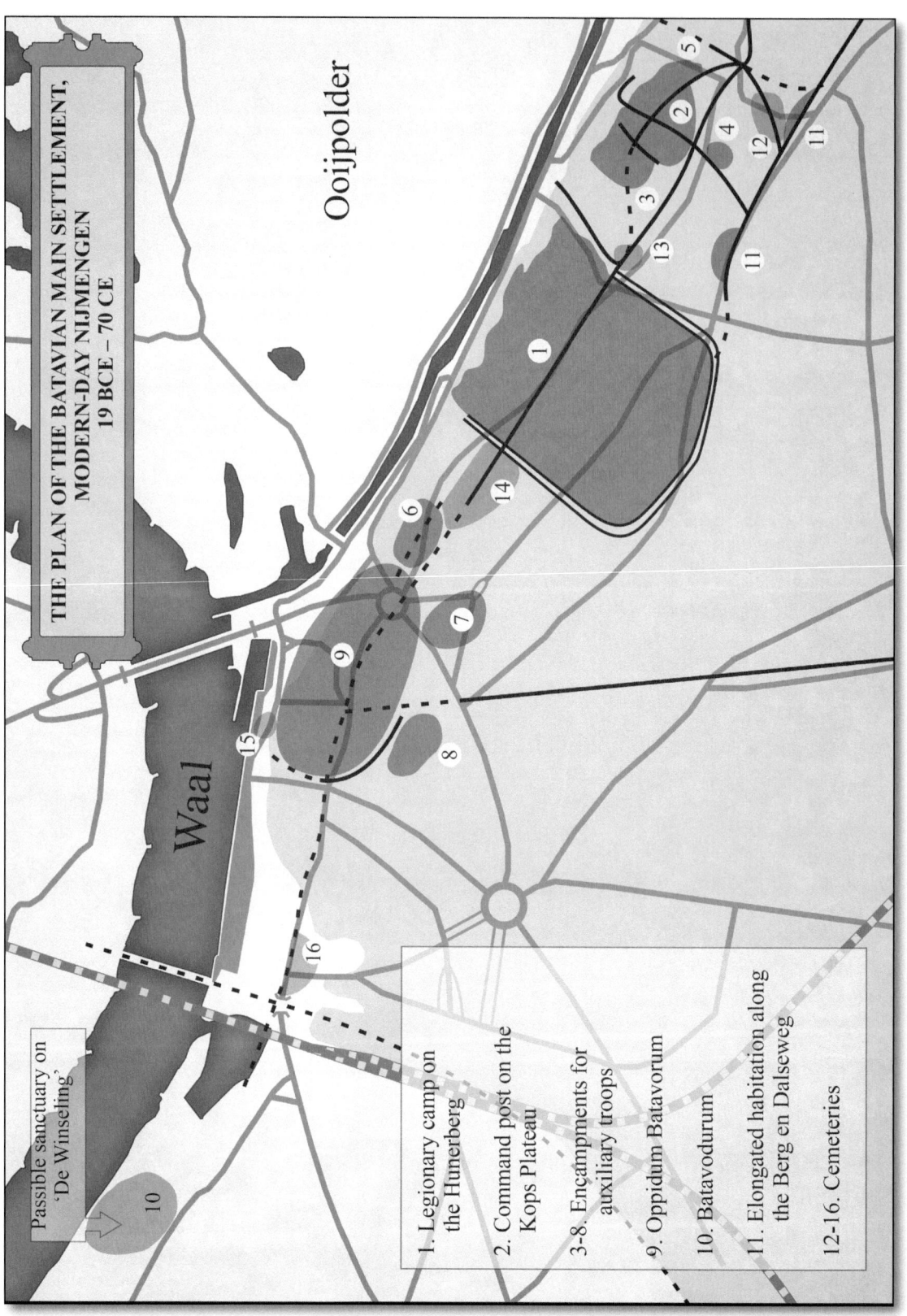

The plan of the Batavian main settlement, modern-day Nijmengen, during the period 19 BC – 70 AD.

burials were uncovered.²³ The Batavian funerary rite, unchanged from the Iron Age, was incineration: the deceased was cremated on a pyre and afterwards the remains were gathered in an urn and buried in the grave. The ritual could, of course, have variations according to personal beliefs or preferences.

At some point in its history, the *oppidum* became *civitas Batavorum*. It is uncertain when this occurred, as historians do not agree on the timing. A victory pillar was erected around 17, most likely to celebrate Germanicus' successes. This point in the settlement's history may have also marked the formal founding of the administrative district. The *summus magistratus*, connected to a *civitas*, was mentioned previously.²⁴ This was a transitional phase. The Batavians had a strong Julian aristocracy, which likely governed the city and promoted Roman-style administration.

A Batavian municipal order with 'tribal' characteristics existed from the time of Drusus onwards.²⁵ One of the main questions is who inhabited Batavodurum at its inception: Batavians or Romans? Archaeologists concluded in the past that the settlement was likely Roman due to its orderly, Roman-like urbanistic structure and the low percentage of locally made pottery. These conclusions are based on excavations of only a small portion of the town's total 20 ha area. There is no reason to question the speed at which the newly established urban elites, along with the former tribal elites, adopted Roman ware and the Empire's easily accessible material culture. The presence of a Julian aristocracy, a magistrate's office, and a public cult among the Batavians

The victory pillar erected in *civitas Batavorum* to celebrate a Roman general's successes. The general could be Germanicus, but he could also be Tiberius (thus dating the pillar earlier in time). It is presented stored and exhibited at the Valkhof Museum.

23 W.J.H. Willems, H. van Enckevort, *Vlpia Noviomagus. Roman Nijmegen. The Batavian capital at the imperial frontier*, JRA Supplementary series, 73, 2009, p. 21.
24 See footnote note 11.
25 Roymans, *Ethnic identity*, p. 202.

would not have been possible without a positive commitment from the native aristocracy.[26] The political agency of the tribal elites had a dual purpose: to gain imperial favour and to attract the general population by presenting themselves as an elite warrior group that provided military services to the Roman emperor and functioned as an intermediary for the wellbeing of the tribe.

After the *oppidum* was granted *civitas* status, it became an important location on the Rhine frontier. In this context, some tribes were clients of the Batavians, who were Rome's strongest ally in the area. The primary tribe in this position were the *Cananefates*, who resided west of the Batavians, in the modern-day Leiden area and along the seashore. According to Tacitus,[27] the Cananefates were related to the Batavians, but their material culture suggests a possible closeness to the Frisians. It is likely that Tacitus considered them related due to their alliance and common Germanic background. The *Cananefates* supported the Batavians during their rebellion against Roman leadership without questioning whether they should also rebel or not. It is possible that members of the *Cananefates*' warriors were part of the pre-revolt Batavian cohorts. Afterwards, they had their own cohort placed in physical proximity to a Batavian cohort and/or the *ala*. It is interesting to note that they do not have a Romanised elite, and their leaders are not officers, retaining their peregrine status. This implies a subordinate relationship with the Batavians, who likely represented their interests to the Romans. During the 2nd century, other tribes such as the *Marsaci*, *Sturii*, and *Frisiavones* may have also been clients of the Batavians. They were included in the recruitment area of the equites singulares from the 2nd century,[28] which likely continued the Julio-Claudian and Flavian tradition of the Batavian guard. However, after the revolt, the Batavians appear to have lost these client tribes from the coast.

The territory of the *civitas* likely encompassed the land of the aforementioned tribes. The forum served as the focal point for displays of imperial loyalty and identity construction. The group of soldiers and ex-soldiers were able to interpret Roman symbolism and decode imperial propaganda messages for their kin who remained at home. In the midst of the rebellion, the leader of the allied *Lingones* ordered the destruction of all *foederis Romani monumenta*.[29] This reference demonstrates the existence of monuments that highlighted loyalty to Rome, as well as their significance in terms of quantity, location, and importance. A similar situation may have occurred within the Batavian region.

In the rural area of the Batavian territory, a shift was identified archaeologically during the late Iron Age and beginning of the Roman period.[30]

---

26 Roymans, *Ethnic identity*, p. 204.
27 Tacitus, *Historiae* IV 15.
28 Roymans, *Ethnic identity*, p. 208.
29 Tacitus, *Historiae* IV 67.
30 D. Habermehl *et. al.*, 'Investigating migration and mobility in the Eraly Roman frontier. The case of the Batavi in the Dutch Rhine Delta (ca. 50-30 BC-AD 40)', *Germania*, 100, 2022, pp. 65-108.

Thus, house architecture as well as pottery have suffered external influences, linking developments with the Dutch northern coast and the German Lippe area. These suggest migrations – which are constantly mentioned in the written Latin sources dealing with this time and space. As well, after the Empire becomes a constant presence, the material culture becomes quickly and heavily influenced by it, and more uniform traditions and forms take root.

At the end of the Julio-Claudian period, Rome referred to this group as Batavians. Although the roots of this term are unknown, the Batavians identified themselves as such with pride. However, identity is a complex concept, as human society shapes itself not only in relation to other groups, but also with its collective consciousness and the sacred.

Hercules Magusanus – the Batavian protector god

A *civitas* generally requires a ruling cult to provide a spiritual sense of belonging. In Roman western Europe, these major local cults were typically a syncretism of pre-existing deities and their Roman counterparts, or the Roman main deity, Jupiter.

The Batavians considered the cult of Hercules Magusanus an emblematic part of their identity from the outset, as it most probably overlapped with a La Tène pre-existing deity of the tribe, for which there is no other direct proof. Hercules Magusanus was a deity worshipped by the Batavians at municipal, military, and private levels, particularly by ex-soldiers, due to its close association with military triumph. The god is emblematic of the Batavians' history and is attested in approximately 20 inscriptions, primarily from Lower Germania, but also from other locations where Batavian troops were stationed, such as Britannia, Dacia and Italy. During the reign of Elagabal (218–222 AD), members of the *equites singulares Augusti* from Rome consecrated an altar to the deity of Germanic origin.[31] The consecrators, who can be identified as Batavians and as coming from the Lower Rhine area, supplementary attest to the deity's Germanic origin. Furthermore, Hercules Magusanus is depicted alongside Hercules Deusoniensis on coin issues of Postumus (260–269 AD), a claimant to the Roman throne who famously emphasised his supposed Batavian ancestry. The detail underscores the regional significance of the Low Germanic deity even during this relatively late period.[32]

---

31 CIL VI 31162.
32 Postumus came from Germania Inferior; whether he was really of Batavian origin, as ancient sources suggest, cannot be determined with certainty. However, he at least wanted to create the appearance of such an origin (B. H. Stolte, 'Die religiösen Verhältnisse in Niedergermanien', in W. Haase (ed.), Aufstieg und Niedergang der römischen Welt, Bd. II 18, 1 Religion (Heidentum: Die religiösen Verhältnisse in den Provinzen) (Berlin, New York 1986), p. 629; G. Elmer, 'Die Münzprägung der gallischen Kaiser von Postumus bis Tetricus in Köln, Trier und Mailand', *BJB*, 146, 1941, pp. 1–106, kat. 558–559).

FORTISSIMI AND VALIDISSIMI: THE BATAVIAN AUXILIARIES OF THE ROMAN ARMY

An *antoninianus* of Postumus with the representation of Hercules Magusanus (from the collection of Yves Gunzenreiner, ex CGB 38, 30 April 2009, 977: https://leunumismatik.com/de/lot/3/340/[3])

Hercules Magusanus was the primary tribal deity of the Batavians, to whom the most significant sanctuaries in the region, such as the Empel temple, were dedicated. The Batavian origin of this Germanic god is considered proven due to the geographic location of the Batavian area and the dedicators, who are often identifiable as Germanic. Additionally, the earliest known inscription featuring the deity originates from the heartland of the Batavians in the Lower Rhine region, specifically from the village of Ruimel in the Nijmegen vicinity, which is situated 10 km away from Empel. The public sanctuaries of Empel and Elst played a key role in the construction and maintaining of Batavian identity.

Modern reconstruction of the temple of Empel.

Sanctuary wall from the temple of Elst (https://www.livius.org/articles/place/elst/).

Regrettably, the gods' iconography lacks indigenous elements and strictly adheres to the canonical Herculean iconography. The deity is depicted holding a club and wearing a lion skin, occasionally accompanied by Cerberus. The reason why Hercules, and not another deity, was linked to the local god is likely due to his masculine virtues. However, unlike Mars, he was also a guardian of livestock and a wandering hero, rather than an exclusively martial god. The legend states that Hercules travelled to the Germanic peoples and became the mythical forbearer of northern barbarians. It was fitting for the descendants of Hercules to supply elite troops and bodyguards for the Julio-Claudian emperors.[33] This likely formed part of Batavian 'intentional history', a mythical variant of their alliance with Rome.

Hercules Magusanus was highly respected by the Batavians throughout the Empire and was considered their tribal god.

Portraits from the beginning

The initial decades of Batavian history can be characterised by their emergence in European history, stepping into their role as a 'martial people', as well as the consecration of their status as strong allies of Rome on the Rhine frontier.

Although we lack concrete biographical data on named individuals from this early times, it is important to mention them with the available details. One such individual is *Chariovalda*,[34] whose Germanic name stands out among the commonly known Greek and Latin names of the Batavians. This is not

---

33   Roymans, *Ethnic identity*, p. 246.
34   Tacitus, *Annales* II 11.

FORTISSIMI AND VALIDISSIMI: THE BATAVIAN AUXILIARIES OF THE ROMAN ARMY

a Batavian from a military family who Latinised his name to fit in, especially in Rome, but an early chieftain who never left his homeland. The name of his eventual sons is unknown. Linguists consider Chariovalda a Latinised form of Harjawalda/Hariwald, providing a glimpse of what Batavian names looked like before full Latinisation.

Who was he? Chariovalda was a Batavian leader who fought in Drusus' campaign against Arminius. Chariovalda died in battle on the Wesser river in 16 BC. He and the Batavians launched a full frontal attack, showcasing their skills in crossing rivers and fighting in harsh conditions. They crossed where the stream was most rapid, taking the Cherusci by surprise. Chariovalda and his men fought bravely in the forest, but he ultimately perished when his horse was killed beneath him. He died surrounded by other tribal chiefs. Some of the Batavian soldiers managed to save themselves 'by their own strength' and with the help of the Roman cavalry. However, their leader and other chiefs bravely fought in the midst of the battle, adding to the Batavians' military reputation.

Although Chariovalda is the first known Batavian leader, it is also worth mentioning a fictional character associated with the Batavians. While anecdotal, this story contributes to the later perception and understanding of the Batavians. The name '*Bato*' was coined by Dutch antiquaries in the early 16th century to provide a focal point and identity for early Batavian histories. According to Gerard Geldenhouwer, Bato led the Batavians to the Dutch river area and founded Batenburg on the Meuse, followed by Nijmegen on the Waal. However, this account is fictional and should be treated as such. P.C. Hooft based his tragedy 'Baeto' on this story.

The first stages of Batavian history are intriguing, as they enter history as warriors, loyal to Rome from the start. Most clues suggest the historical Batavi were formed by a hard nucleus of *Chatti* warriors who migrated into a part of the territory formerly administered by the *Eburones* and mixed with the remains of the local population. Who were these migrants? Mostly warriors, cavalrymen and their families. It is hard to say if their migration is to be overlapped with dissensions within the *Chatti* tribe, but the quickness with which the Batavian identity was assumed and the loyalty proven towards Rome suggest that this group was given much more by the Roman Empire compared to what they have had at home, in terms of status and maybe living conditions.

We do not see any major identity shift in time, only the consolidation of their image and their place within the Roman Empire and its army. However, there may have been underlying issues in the seemingly perfect relationship between the emperors of Rome and their loyal Germanic soldiers, as the year 69 violently brings about the next stage of Batavian history: the rebellion that ravaged the north of the Empire and ultimately proved the bilateral need to continue together.

2

Historical Turning Point: The Batavian Rebellion

Despite (or perhaps because of) their exceptional status, in 69 AD the Batavians were the protagonists of one of the fiercest rebellions the Roman Empire faced in the 1st century AD.

Led by a Romanised aristocrat (Julius Civilis), the Batavians and their allies defied and challenged Roman rule over the Lower Rhine territories. Various episodes of the rebellion are known to historians, described in literature and revealed by archaeology, so that today we have the possibility of reconstructing a coherent history and understanding the Batavians' motives (which are not beyond controversy), as well as their fighting tactics. Having become a real threat to the Empire, Civilis entered into peace talks in the spring of 70 AD and the Batavians were subsequently reintegrated into the Roman fold. Apparently, Vespasian's ascension to the throne helped, as Vitellius had personally antagonised the Rhine tribes, being a cruel and mediocre commander for the Germanic armies.

The Batavians had been loyal allies of the Romans for many years, and their warriors had fought alongside Roman legions in numerous campaigns. However, tensions began to rise when the Emperor Nero committed suicide in 68 AD, leading to a power vacuum and a period of political instability in Rome.

The Year of the Four Emperors

The Senate proclaimed Galba, the elderly governor of Hispania Tarraconenisis, emperor. He was supported by the Praetorian guard who had betrayed Nero. To add insult to injury, Galba disbanded the Germanic guard and sent them home because of their loyalty to Nero. They certainly didn't return home happy, even if they were financially compensated. In this context, the *Batavi*, already dissatisfied with their treatment by the Roman authorities, saw an opportunity to assert their independence and rebelled against Roman rule. The year of the four emperors was thus also the year of the Batavian revolt.

Galba was not popular for long: paranoid, the new emperor began to execute suspected conspirators without a trial, just like his predecessor. Thus Salvius Otho, another senator, bribed the praetorians once again, making them assassinate Galba in the *forum* and proclaim Otho himself emperor. But in the meanwhile, the Germanic troops had already refused to swear allegiance to Galba and had proclaimed their commander, Aulus Vitellius, emperor. Vitellius marched on Italy with one of the Empire's best armies, forged in the Germanic wars, and defeated Otho, although he tried to negotiate peace. On the banks of the river Po, the Batavian cohorts clashed with an army supporting the emperor anointed as such in Rome. A unit of gladiators in small boats went on to occupy an island in the middle of the river, which would have given a tactic advantage to the ones holding it. As a side note, incorporating gladiators in the army was a sign of huge despair from the part of the new and ephemeral emperor: besides physical qualities and some battle training, the gladiators were only prepared for fights in the arena, had absolutely no military training and no experience in acting together, as a cluster unit. As the gladiators were rowing, the Batavians swam to the island with all their weapons, got there first and annihilated Otho's force.[1] Otho committed suicide and Vitellius seemed to be sole emperor, recognised as such by the Senate. But the commander of the army of Judaea, Titus Flavius Vespasianus, backed by both Eastern and Danubian armies, challenged Vitellius' claimed and was himself proclaimed emperor, the fourth of the year 69.

After occupying Rome, Vitellius sent back some of the units that had fought for him, including the Batavian infantry (the cohorts). Before they had even arrived home, their orders were changed and they were summoned to return to Italy to assist Vitellius in his forthcoming battle against Vespasian.

Portrait of emperor Vespasian, now in the collection of the Musei Capitolini. (https://www.thecollector.com/vespasian-emperor/)

Vitellius even instructed the commander of the Rhine army, Marcus Hordeonius Flaccus, to send additional troops. Our main source for the events of 69 and 70, Tacitus' Histories, portrays Flaccus in a very negative light, as an incompetent defeatist, while idealising the Batavian leader Julius Civilis as a courageous and moral fighter. Although it is possible that Flaccus was truly incompetent, he at least sensed that the Batavians were becoming restless and anticipated trouble. As a result, he refused to comply to Vitellius' request, recognising that it was unwise to send more soldiers away from the frontier. Given Flaccus' arguments, Vitellius ordered new soldiers to be recruited as a deterrent to future rebellions, but this measure failed to impress the Batavians as there were no troops nearby to enforce the threat. Tacitus

---

1   Tacitus, *Historiae* II 35.

says[2] that the Batavians didn't like the idea, but what really did the damage was the greed, corruption and debauchery of the recruiting officers. A passing remark of Tacitus underlines the rift that these officers created between the Romans and their Batavian allies. The writer says that the Roman recruiting official took away Batavian boys 'to satisfy their lust' (*ad stuprum*).[3] Obviously, this was unacceptable behaviour, as Rome was not at war with the Batavians at the time, on the contrary, they were allies and free men. Civilis will stress on this, among other abuses, in order to underline that the Romans got to the point of treating their northern allies as slaves.

As we saw in the previous chapter, the Batavian population was not very large. Demographic research has led to the conclusion that every Batavian family had at least one son in the army. Recruiting more men was almost impossible, and it is not surprising that the old, the unfit and the extremely young were called up for recruitment.

This was the match that ignited the rebellion.

The leaders

Our knowledge of the barbarian leaders is very much linked to the rebellion, we don't have Arminius-type biographies for them, we don't know exactly where they came from or what happened to them afterwards.

Julius Civilis was the central figure in the rebellion, a Roman citizen and, it seems, a member of the old tribal royalty (*regia stirpe*). He had fought in one of the Batavian auxiliary units of the Roman army during Claudius' invasion of Britain – this is a detail of importance. In 68, Julius Civilis and his brother Julius Paulus were arrested on charges of treason, although Tacitus believes the charges were trumped up. Julius Paulus was executed, while Civilis was pardoned by emperor Galba. However, Civilis was arrested again in late 68. This time there was evidence that Civilis had indeed been involved in a conspiracy. Nevertheless, Vitellius pardoned him in an attempt to win the support of the eight Batavian cohorts, and this strategy proved successful, as the soldiers eventually sided with Vitellius and joined his march on Rome, as we have previously mentioned.

The Batavians had reasons to be unhappy with Rome and the imperial power's handling of their allegiance, and Civilis' personal reasons overlapped perfectly with the tribe's discontent. Julius Civilis had two possible reasons for his actions. First, Tacitus notes that the execution of his brother was a strong personal motive for revenge – perfectly understandable on a human

---

2   Tacitus, *Historiae* IV 14.
3   For more on martial rape in the Roman world in general and on what these actions specifically meant in the context of the Batavian rebellion, see I. Clegg, 'Martial rape and the Batavian revolt. Shameful behaviour', *Ancient warfare*, XV/2, 2022, pp. 21–23.

level. Second, as a member of a leading Batavian family, Civilis may have been motivated to restore the royal power of his ancestors. Although Tacitus does not explicitly mention it, it is possible that Civilis considered it at some point, as we will see. Tacitus reports a speech by Civilis in which he claims that the Romans treated the Batavians as subjects rather than allies, citing corrupt officers and harsh recruitment practices as evidence. However, it is uncertain whether Civilis actually made this speech. It is possible that Tacitus invented it, as he often focused on the corruption of Roman officials.

Tacitus considered that the claimed rebellion against Vitellius, and not the Empire, was a post-factum fake. However, it is unclear whether the Batavians were truly fighting for freedom. The storyline of the revolt makes it difficult to determine. Drawing a parallel with Arminius, who apparently really was focused on independence, it seems that not really, that the Batavians rather desired fair treatment and high status under a benevolent Roman emperor.

Civilis was the leader of the rebellion, but other figures also played important roles. **Veleda**, the priestess, had a religious aura and was probably extremely influential in motivating the Batavians to go to war. The origin of the name Veleda is uncertain, and it appears to be a title rather than a name. While some have suggested that it comes from the Celtic word 'veleta', meaning 'prophetess', the region where she lived was not a Celtic-speaking one. Another possible origin is the West-Germanic word 'waldon', meaning 'to have power'. It is uncertain whether Veleda merely prophesied success or actively encouraged the Batavians during their rebellion against the Roman Empire in 69. Unfortunately, details about her life are scarce. Tacitus[4] describes Veleda as an unmarried woman with significant influence, particularly over the *Bructeri* tribe.

It is important to note that when the Batavians captured the Roman navy's flagship, they towed it up the Lippe River to present it to Veleda, who lived in a large tower near the river. This action suggests that she was actively supporting the rebellion. Veleda's authority was unquestioned and widespread, as evidenced by the inhabitants of the Roman city of Cologne accepting her arbitration in a conflict with the *Tencteri*, a tribe from free Germania. Following the suppression of the Batavian revolt, Veleda was either captured by the Romans or she willingly sought asylum with them.

Another figure of the rebellion is **Brinno**, the leader of the *Cannanefates*, whom Tacitus unceremoniously referred to as 'foolish'. According to Tacitus, Brinno's father had been hostile towards the Romans during the reign of Caligula, which may have determined Brinno's designation as leader in times of revolt. Brinno was selected to lead the *Cannanefates* in their rebellion against Rome and he was ceremoniously raised on a shield in this context. Brinno's first successful move as commander was to attack

---

4   Tacitus, *Historiae* IV 61.

Roman winter camps by the sea with the help of the *Frisii*, catching the unprepared enemy off guard.[5]

Another complex figure, about whom more information would have been crucial for our understanding of his actions and background motivations, is **Claudius Labeo**, the Batavian commander of the *ala* stationed near Nijmegen on the Kops Plateau, who was initially loyal to the Romans. During the early stages of the revolt, when the Romans invaded the Nijmegen area, general Flaccus relied on Labeo's *ala* and was confident of his loyalty due to an old rivalry he had with Civilis, which seemed to be extremely bitter. However, Labeo and his cavalry defected, resulting in the heavy defeat of the Romans.[6] Despite this, Civilis did not trust Labeo and exiled him under guard among the Frisians. Labeo escaped and sided with the Romans again, leading a guerrilla war against the *Cannanefates* and the *Marsaci*, who were the Batavians' allies. This caused Civilis to divide his forces,[7] and thus Labeo's actions, prompted by the rebellion leader's hate towards him, played a crucial role in the ultimate Roman triumph. However, his fate after the war is unknown.

On the Roman side, the leadership was markedly different, but a few individuals played more prominent roles in the course of events.

Marcus Hordeonnius Flaccus, a senator, commanded the Rhine army when the rebellion began. Tacitus paints a grim picture of his leadership. Before the rebellion broke out, he realised that the area was not peaceful and was hesitant to disperse his troops. Following the forced recruitments and the onset of the rebellion, Flaccus did not react promptly. However, he may have taken some time to assess whether he was facing a small local revolt or a civil war and whether his opponents were truly supporting Vespasian. In the latter scenario, the general's position would have been quite complicated. Nevertheless, he engaged in battle against the Batavians with varying degrees of success. At a certain point, the eight well-trained Batavian cohorts decided to return home, and Flaccus, who was in Germania Superior at the time, did not destroy them but allowed them to return to their homeland. Tacitus criticises him as weak, but he may have simply preferred to keep the troubles at the periphery and push them away from Gallia Belgica. He reinforced Xanten and indeed Civilis laid siege to it, but even smarter, the Batavian made his men swear alliance to Vespasian – which rendered Flaccus' position impossible. Afterwards, he travelled to Bonn[8] where the situation became complicated and the local legion rejected Flaccus' command, which he wisely accepted. That he was not a popular figure is at least sure and Tacitus' depiction might have been based on contemporary depictions and impressions. In November, Vespasian

---

5   Tacitus, *Historiae* IV 15.
6   Tacitus, *Historiae* IV 18.
7   Tacitus, *Historiae* IV 56.
8   Tacitus, *Historiae* IV 26.

defeated Vitellius' Germanic troops and Flaccus swore allegiance to the new emperor. Civilis revealed his true intentions by attacking the Roman conjoined armies of Flaccus and Vocula at Krefeld, even after the ascension of the new emperor. However, he was ultimately defeated. Flaccus held a favourable position as he restored Bonn, Cologne, Neuss, and Xanten. However, on the night of Saturnalia (17 December), he was attacked and killed by his own soldiers. This murder boosted Civilis' confidence, and the rebellion continued for a few more months.

Quintus Petillius Cerialis is the general that won the war for Rome, defeating the Batavians in the end. Coming from an important family, Cerialis, aged around 30, was commander of a legion in Britannia during Boudica's revolt. It is recorded that Cerialis suffered a disastrous defeat by the *Iceni* at some point,[9] but he also achieved successes as his career progressed. At one stage, he married Domitilla, the only daughter of the future emperor Vespasian. Although she died before her father ascended the imperial throne, Cerialis' connection to the family remained strong. Cerialis was sent to appease the already complicated and embarrassing Rhine rebellion, which was a sign of great trust. He fulfilled his duty well and subsequently returned to Britannia as governor. After leaving the island, it is likely that he spent the rest of his life in Rome or at a nearby estate, passing away at the age of approximately 65.[10]

Storyline of the rebellion. The first stages

As we have seen, there are several potential motives for Julius Civilis and the Batavians' revolt against Rome, which may conflict with each other. Firstly, Civilis may have sought revenge for his brother's execution. Additionally, as a member of the leading Batavian family, he may have desired the restoration of royal power that his ancestors once held. Although the Batavians had potentially conflicting motivations, they were united by their bitter resentment towards the recent oppressive recruitment practices of the Romans. It is worth mentioning that these were short-term motives and recent malcontents. In the end, the fact that there were no real transgenerational deeply rooted problems – on the contrary, it seems – made the return to the Roman fold possible so quickly after the rebellion.

Just before the rebellion began, Julius Civilis was still in command of one of the Batavian auxiliary units in Roman service. The commander of the Rhine army, Marcus Hordeonius Flaccus, was unaware that Civilis was conspiring against Rome, although he sensed that something was amiss. Civilis took advantage of this and incited the *Cananefates* to revolt, hoping

---

9   Tacitus, *Annales* XIV 32.
10 v. Cerealis, Petillius, in *Encyclopædia Britannica, vol. 5 (11th ed.)* (Cambridge: Cambridge University Press, 1910–1911), p. 760.

HISTORICAL TURNING POINT: THE BATAVIAN REBELLION

that Flaccus would send him to suppress the rebellion. Thus began the conflict between the Romans and Brinno, in August 69, when Brinno destroyed two auxiliary camps, one of which has been identified as Praetorium Agrippinae (modern day Valkenburg, NL). Brinno then threatened to attack other Roman forts in the region, prompting the Romans to burn them down out of fear of being unable to defend them. Among the forts destroyed by the Romans was Traiectum, which is modern-day Utrecht.[11] According to Tacitus, under the leadership of Aquilius, a senior centurion, the headquarters of multiple auxiliary units and other troops from the region regrouped in the east. However, their army was only a theoretical concept as they lacked substantial military might. This was not surprising considering Vitellius had withdrawn most of the units' active personnel. Fortuitously, the identity of Aquilius has been revealed through an archaeological discovery: a small silver disk[12] was found in the cavalry base, located east of the Batavian capital, *oppidum Batavorum*, on the Kops Plateau.

Small silver disk dating from the time of the rebellion and mentioning centurion Aquilius' name. It is now stored in the Valkhof Museum.

The disk, meant to be attached to a wooden chest or something similar as a name tag, confirms that the man's name was Caius Aquillius Proculus, and he was affiliated with the VIII Augusta legion, which was not typically stationed in the Germanic provinces. This finding is significant as it provides support for the Roman general Flaccus, whom Tacitus so harshly judges. The now undoubtable presence of senior centurion Aquilius in Nijmegen suggests that Flaccus had already called for reinforcements, indicating that he anticipated potential trouble among the Batavians. Thus, Tacitus' narrative that Brinno's attack was entirely unexpected is somewhat misleading. Although the Romans were caught off-guard by the Cananefatian revolt, they were well aware of the rising tensions in the region.

Civilis employed a deceptive strategy by criticising the Roman commanders for abandoning their forts and offering to handle the *Cananefates'* uprising personally with the aid of his own unit, while suggesting that the Roman commanders return to their stations. However, the Germans were fond of fighting among themselves and could not keep the plan a secret for long. Clues regarding the scheme began to surface, indicating that Civilis' advice was part of a deception: the dispersed units were more susceptible to elimination, and Brinno was not the instigator or the driving force behind the uprising, but rather Civilis himself was.

Tacitus presents a biased viewpoint by omitting any mention of the Roman commander who uncovered Civilis' stratagem and investigated the situation. It is probable that the individual who discovered the plan

---

11   Tacitus, *Historiae* IV 15.
12   AE 1998, 966.

held a higher rank than Civilis in the military hierarchy, such as Marcus Hordeonius Flaccus. After his real plan became known, Civilis turned to force and divided the Cananefatians, Frisians, and Batavians into separate combat units. Meanwhile, the Romans established a front near the Rhine and deployed naval vessels from the area to face the enemy. The battle was brief, as a Tungrian unit defected to Civilis' side, causing the Roman troops to scatter and succumb to the joint attack of allies and foes. This desertion must have been concerning to the Romans because it implied that auxiliary units recruited from otherwise loyal tribes could be untrustworthy in the context of local turbulences. However, due to the depleted legions, Flaccus had no choice but to deploy them in battle anyway.

Civilis' triumph immediately boosted the rebels' prestige and laid a solid foundation for future action. They acquired the necessary arms and ships and were hailed as liberators, causing the news to spread throughout the Germanic and Gallic provinces. The former promptly offered assistance, while Civilis used deceit and bribery to form an alliance with the Gallic provinces. He returned captured commanders to their respective communities and gave soldiers the choice of discharge on honourable terms or continued service. As a result, the Romans were compelled to withdraw from the regions surrounding the Maas, Waal, and Rhine rivers. The Kops Plateau, a Roman cavalry base, is the only camp in the region that lacks a burning layer, indicating that the Romans were able to maintain control of it and the Waal crossing near Nijmegen.

Previously, the rebelling allies had only fought against Roman auxiliaries. However, Flaccus managed to rally the Vth Alaudae and the XVth Primigenia legions, along with three auxiliary units consisting of Ubians, Trevirans, and even a Batavian squadron. It may seem questionable to trust a Batavian unit (specifically the one from Kops Plateau) in this situation, and it seems that Flaccus did indeed misjudge the men he was dealing with. The squadron in question was the *ala*, commanded by Claudius Labeo. It seems that Labeo and Civilis had a past conflict and actively disliked each other. The two armies faced each other in the Nijmegen area, but the Roman left front was quickly exposed by the defection of the Batavian cavalry regiment. Despite this setback, the legionaries were able to maintain their ranks and protect their arms. The Ubian and Treverian auxiliaries fled in disarray, leaving the legions exposed to the brunt of the Batavian attack. The defeat of the Roman legionary army by the Batavians was a significant blow to Roman prestige and a great success for Julius Civilis and his rebel forces.

Consequently, the Batavians were able to take over the Kops Plateau, which was the last Roman garrison in their land. Julius Civilis and the Batavian army have achieved significant success in their rebellion. They defeated two Roman legions and expelled the Romans from the region along the rivers Maas, Waal, and Rhine. They formed alliances with neighbouring tribes and gained recognition as the most powerful tribe in the area. The victory not only avenged Civilis' brother but also provided him with an opportunity to become the undisputed leader of his tribe. His success in war earned him prestige, making him a strong candidate for the position of king. However, it is unclear if he ever pursued this goal.

The Batavians had gained their independence, and they believed that the Romans would acknowledge it. According to reports, Civilis had in his possession a letter from Vespasian, the commander of the Roman forces in Judaea who had rebelled against emperor Vitellius, urging Civilis, with whom he had fought during the wars in Britannia, to revolt. This would have prevented Vitellius from using all his troops against Vespasian. At this point, Civilis had fulfilled Vespasian's request, albeit for his own reasons. The Batavians might have hoped that their independence would be acknowledged by Vespasian, as Tiberius had granted autonomy to the Frisians and *Chauci* in a similar situation in 28. It is possible that the letter never existed and was a mere fabrication, but this story was circulated during the revolt and it played its part in the rebels' propaganda.

Into the heat of the battle

Julius Civilis had achieved everything he wanted. However, within weeks, he made a fateful decision that would ultimately lead to his downfall. The Batavians should not have attacked the base of the two Roman legions at Castra Vetera (Xanten), as any attack on this symbol of Roman power would prompt a large army to retaliate. Even if the civil war *was* over, the victor would be obliged to punish the attackers. The memory of the Jews' attack on the XIIth Fulminata, almost three years prior was still vivid, as well as Rome's resentment. Julius Civilis, a Roman citizen who had served in the Roman auxiliaries, would undoubtedly have been aware of this. However, in September 69, the Batavians attacked Xanten despite the potential consequences. The timing was opportune, as the army of the Danube had just sided with Vespasian and now posed a threat to Italy, meaning that any serious Roman retaliation would be postponed. Julius Civilis dyed his hair red and swore to let it grow until he had destroyed the two legions. The reason for his extreme actions remains a mystery, but they may suggest that he was still mainly fighting for revenge and grief rather than following a calculated strategic plan.

The Batavians were well prepared for the attack, as the eight units who had fought for Vitellius in Italy in the spring were now back home. The commander of the Roman forces in Germania Superior and Germania Inferior, Marcus Hordeonius Flaccus, permitted the eight Batavian auxiliary units to pass through Mainz. Although he initially considered using force to bring them under control, he ultimately decided against it, as we have seen. The reasoning was sound. However, once the seasoned units arrived, Civilis assumed command of a proper army.

The refusal of the two legions at Xanten to accept the oath of allegiance to Vespasian and their continuous loyalty to Vitellius added to the fuel of the Batavian rebellion. Civilis, along with the *Bructeri* and *Tencteri* tribes, launched a full-scale attack on Xanten. The siege lasted for several months,

FORTISSIMI AND VALIDISSIMI: THE BATAVIAN AUXILIARIES OF THE ROMAN ARMY

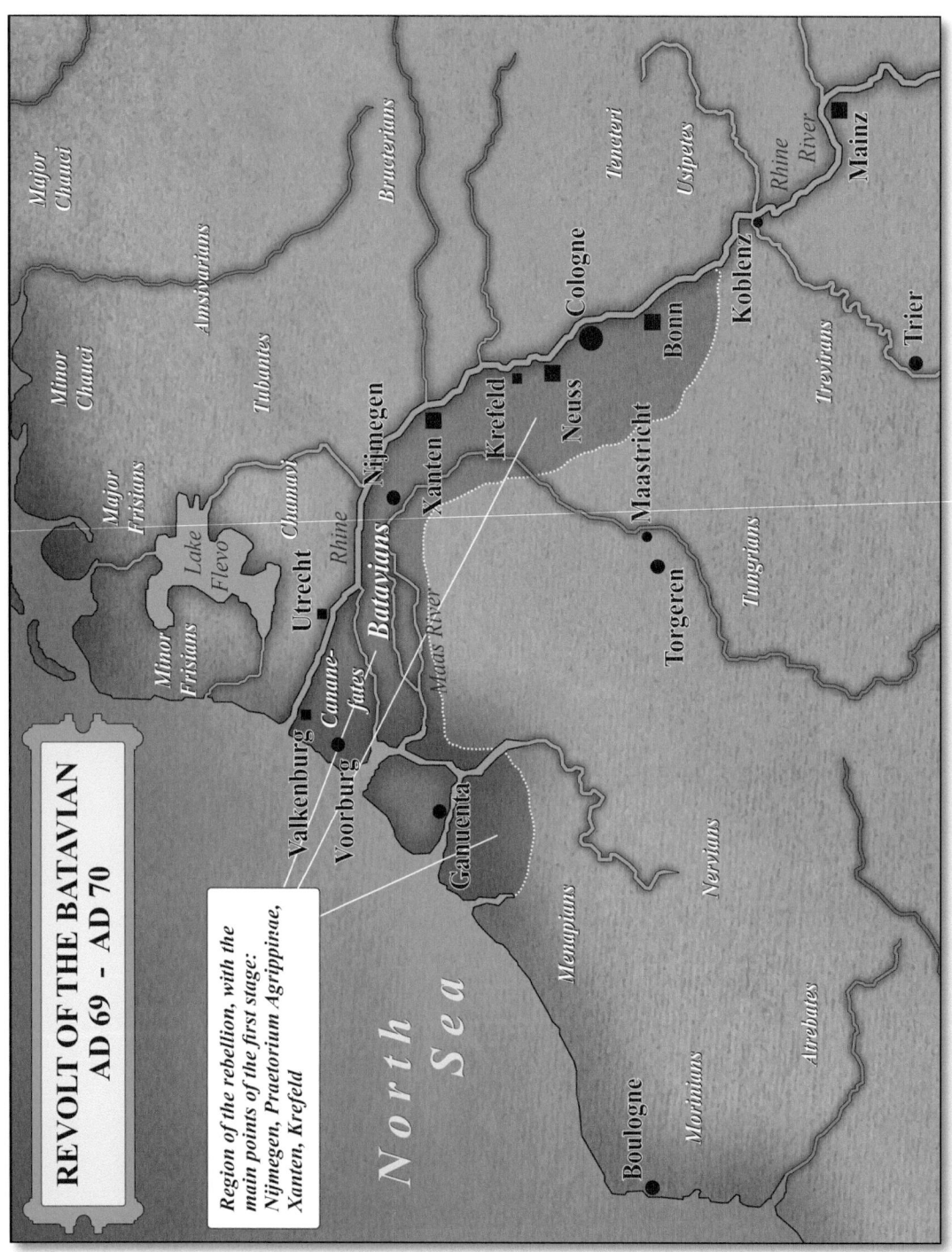

Map of the region of the rebellion, with the main points of the first stage and troops movements: Nijmegen, Praetorium Agrippinae, Xanten, Krefeld

HISTORICAL TURNING POINT: THE BATAVIAN REBELLION

during which time the Roman garrison was cut off from all supplies and reinforcements. However, Munius Lupercus, the Roman commander at Xanten, demonstrated his skilled strategic abilities by successfully holding out against the Batavian forces. He maintained high morale among his troops and coordinated successful sorties against the besiegers. Despite being outnumbered, the Roman defenders held out for several months. The Batavians, unable to launch a full-scale assault, resorted to a blockade, cutting off the Roman supply lines in hopes of starving the legions into submission. The situation in Xanten became critical as the defenders resorted to eating their horses. The Romans were struggling to devise a plan to break the siege. Munius Lupercus proposed a daring plan to attack the Batavian camp while their forces were divided. He suggested that half of the Roman troops launch a surprise attack on the Batavian camp, while the other half remain in Xanten to defend it. The Roman commanders had few options and agreed to Lupercus' risky plan. The attack was launched and caught the Batavians off guard, resulting in initial success for the Romans. However, the Batavians quickly regrouped and counter-attacked, driving the Romans back to Xanten with heavy losses. The failure of this attack dealt a severe blow to the morale of the Roman defenders, but despite this setback, Munius Lupercus managed to rally the troops and maintain their spirits.

Meanwhile, Flaccus called for military action and successfully gathered the I Germanica from Bonn, the XXII Primigenia under the command of Gaius Dilius Vocula, and the XVI Gallica. However, a significant shift in the Empire's political situation occurred simultaneously. In November 69, Vespasian marched on Italy and defeated Vitellius, causing a wave of defections among Vitellius' supporters, including some of the Batavian troops besieging Xanten. Flaccus and Vocula found themselves in a difficult situation when Civilis claimed to be fighting for Vespasian, while they had been fighting for their legitimate emperor, Vitellius, up until that point. The commanders administered a new oath of allegiance but had to wait.

Flaccus and Vocula were left uncertain of what to do while waiting at Gelduba (modern Krefeld). If Julius Civilis was truly supporting Vespasian, if the letter indeed existed, then the war would be over as the Rhine army had already sided with Vespasian. However, if Civilis had only pretended to support Vespasian, the war would continue, and the Romans would have had to fight against neighbouring tribes. Several days passed without any word from the north, and Flaccus realised that the Batavian army intended to continue the fight.

Arrow heads (https://www.livius.org/pictures/germany/xanten-cut/vetera-i/xanten-furstenberg-arrowheads/) and catapults (https://www.livius.org/pictures/germany/xanten-cut/vetera-i/xanten-furstenberg-catapult-stones/) from Xanten.

Civilis understood that he had to destroy the army at Krefeld before it joined forces with the besieged. He was aware that the Romans would retaliate after the attack on Xanten, but he also knew that it would take them six months to send an army across the Alps due to the approaching winter. If he could destroy the army at Krefeld, he could take Xanten and expand the rebellious region. Civilis was already negotiating with the Trevirans, who would support him if the Roman forces retreated to Mainz. The fall of Mainz was inevitable if the Batavians and Trevirans worked together. However, Civilis encountered a problem: the army of Flaccus and Vocula, although consisting of three weakened legions, was too large to confront in a conventional battle. The Batavians attempted to catch the Roman army off-guard by attacking during the night, but the Basque units that Flaccus had called upon arrived in time to turn the tide of the battle. The Basques, known for their ferocity, were able to break through the Batavian lines, inspiring the Roman legions to counter-attack and break the siege. As a result, the Batavian army was forced to retreat. Archaeological evidence attests to the battle at Krefeld, which resulted in a large mass grave for both men and horses.

The remaining Batavian forces, now outnumbered by the Roman defenders, lifted the siege on Castra Vetera and retreated. It is worth noting that Tacitus does not mention the eight Batavian cohorts anymore after this point. Although the siege of Xanten had ended, the Roman victory was a Pyrrhic one,[13] as the defenders had suffered heavy losses and the revolt in Germania continued to rage on.

The triumph at Xanten marked a pivotal moment in the era, demonstrating the Roman army's continued ability to win battles and inspiring hope among other Roman commanders facing similar revolts throughout the Empire. Additionally, the victory showcased the Roman army's capacity to collaborate with foreign allies, such as the Basques, to achieve success, even if they were fighting against some of their most valuable auxiliaries.

Following the victories of Krefeld and Xanten, the Romans withdrew to Neuss to celebrate their success, including the Saturnalia festival. Although Flaccus appeared to have improved his relationship with the troops, even distributing money to celebrate Vespasian's ascension, he was murdered by his soldiers during the Saturnalia celebrations in a drunken riot.[14] If Vocula had not escaped from the camp disguised as a slave, he would have faced the same fate, even if the sources depict him as a well-respected commander. The attack on the two commanders remains a mystery, leaving

---

13 The expression means a victory with losses so high, that it resembles defeat. It comes from King Pyrrhus' of Epirus victory over the Romans, in 279 BC, which was so devastating for the victors, that the king allegedly exclaimed: 'If we win one more fights with the Romans, we will be completely ruined' (Plutarch, *Pyrrhus* XXI 9).

14 Tacitus, *Historiae* IV 36.

room for speculation. As previously mentioned, the Roman expeditionary force had returned to the south, taking troops from Xanten. According to Tacitus, those who remained behind felt betrayed, which is understandable as they were left to deal with the defeated Batavians while the main force was elsewhere. It is possible that the murder was not a result of drunken frenzy, but instead an act of 'fragging', meaning the intentional killing of a commander who was reckless with his soldiers' lives. Alternatively, it could have been a result of Flaccus' (and possibly Vocula's) genuine Vitellian association, or of a more complex plot.

At this point, all theories are equally plausible. However, it is a fact that the defeated Batavians had another opportunity as the Roman Rhine army found itself in disarray once again.

The Gallic Empire and the fall of Xanten

At the beginning of 70 AD, the Empire was off to a promising start: the civil war was over, Vitellius had died, the newly crowned emperor Vespasian was benevolent, and plans were afoot to end the Jewish war and the Batavian revolt. However, the pressing issue was whether the expeditionary force dispatched across the Alps would arrive on time to prevent the situation north of Mainz from worsening. Unfortunately, the Roman reinforcements arrived too late.

The killing of Marcus Hordeonius Flaccus boosted the morale of the defeated rebels. Julius Civilis resumed the siege of the V Alaudae and XV Primigenia in Xanten. The Trevirans and *Lingones*, Gallic tribes living in the Moselle and Upper Rhine regions who had been Romanised, also revolted when they saw the legions' inability to deal effectively with the situation. The previous defeats of the Batavians restored some Roman prestige, but the renewed siege of Xanten by Julius Civilis and the evident discord among the Roman legionaries eliminated the last shred of doubt for the Trevirans and *Lingones*.

The last successful Roman effort was the rescue of Mainz, which was garrisoned by the IV Macedonica and the XXII Primigenia legions at the time. However, when the escaped Gaius Dillius Vocula attempted to aid the Xanten garrison, his Treviran and Lingonian auxiliaries deserted him. Julius Classicus, commander of the Treviran cavalry regiment within the Roman army, exchanged messages with Civilis, as well as with Julius Tutor and Julius Sabinus, a Treviran and a Lingon, respectively. Classicus stated his prestigious lineage, while Sabinus claimed to be the descendant of a woman who was Julius Caesar's mistress during the Gallic War.

The Trevirans and Lingones, unlike the Batavians, were fully Romanised and aimed to establish their own empire, the Gallic Empire. When Vocula realised that Classicus and Tutor were betraying Rome, he retreated to Neuss, and the Gauls encamped nearby. Soldiers from both sides engaged in trade and negotiations, which resulted in a dishonourable agreement where the Roman army pledged allegiance to the Gallic Empire and promised to kill or imprison their commanders. Subsequently, Tutor attacked Cologne and Mainz, while Classicus unsuccessfully attempted to convince the garrison at Xanten to surrender. However, the commander, Munius Lupercus, refused to comply. The I and XVI legions, demoralised, surrendered to the Gallic Empire and were directed to Trier, as they were not fully trusted by the area's atypical emperor, Julius Sabinus. However, Sabinus was an unsuccessful leader, and his war against the *Sequani*, which was supposed to confirm his leadership position, failed. In an attempt to fake his own death, he set fire to the farmhouse where he was hiding. Apparently, he lived in hiding for a rather long time after this strange event, but the idea of a so-called Gallic Empire came to an end. The Trevirans and *Lingones* were eventually invited by the Gauls to cease their aggression, and both tribes, having compromised their relationship with Rome, subsequently sided with Civilis.

After the fragmentation of the Roman army in the north of Mainz, the two legions under siege at Xanten, V Alaudae and XV Primigenia, were ultimately defeated. In March 70, their leader, Munius Lupercus, finally surrendered. The besieged troops found themselves in a difficult situation, torn between loyalty and the desire for survival. They faced hunger and starvation as all their normal and emergency rations had been depleted. In the face of extreme privation, they were forced to resort to eating mules, horses, and other animals that were available, regardless of how unclean or revolting they were. When even these sources of food were exhausted, they had no choice but to eat shrubs, roots, and the grass between the stones. This is a testament to their endurance[15] and loyalty to Rome's ideals.

Eventually, Lupercus sent envoys to Civilis, pleading for their lives. Civilis demanded an oath of allegiance to the Gallic empire before he entertained their request. Overseers were appointed to ensure that the garrison left behind their money and baggage before departing. However, the Germans ambushed them when they were about eight kilometres from Xanten. Many soldiers fell in battle, while others managed to flee back to the camp. Civilis protested and blamed the Germanic allies for their breach of faith, but it is unclear whether this was mere hypocrisy or whether he was unable to control his ferocious allies. The camp was plundered, and the remaining soldiers perished in the flames.

After fulfilling his vow to annihilate the legions from Xanten, Civilis shaved off his long beard and hair. He is said to have given some of the prisoners to his young son to use as targets for his arrows and spears – and there may be some truth in this wild claim, as Tacitus' portrait of the Batavian leader is generally far from negative, while this act denotes pure cruelty, beyond the strict necessities of war. Munius Lupercus, the brave legionary commander, was sent as a gift to Veleda, the divine prophetess, but was executed before he reached her.

Julius Civilis and his Treviran ally, Julius Classicus, took advantage of the opportunity to move to Cologne, which was left unguarded after their victory

---

15   Tacitus, *Historiae* IV 60–61.

HISTORICAL TURNING POINT: THE BATAVIAN REBELLION

over the Romans. However, instead of sacking the city, Civilis chose to make it his headquarters. This was a token of gratitude to its inhabitants, who had apparently sheltered and protected his son. Coins were minted to commemorate the destruction of the V Alaudae and the XV Primigenia.

After the emperor of the Gallic Empire disappeared, the Batavians became the most powerful force in northwest Europe. In the following months they tried to conquer the Romanised tribes of northern Gaul. Civilis invited several Germanic tribes from across the Rhine to join them in looting Gallia Belgica, and these tribes eagerly accepted the invitation. As always, Civilis was also motivated by personal reasons: Labeo, the former commander of the Batavian cavalry who had been despised by Civilis and exiled to the Frisian territories despite having helped him win a battle, had escaped and, with the help of Gaius Dillius Vocula, now a general, had formed a small army which attacked the Batavian and Cananefatian homelands from the south. Civilis aimed to end the guerrilla war and satisfy the Batavian people by defeating Labeo's army. The two armies clashed near the bridge of Trajectum ad Mosam (Maastricht). Civilis encountered resistance in his advance from Claudius Labeo and his irregular force made up of *Baetasii*, Tungrians, and Nervians. Nonetheless, the battle was even until the Batavians swam the river and attacked from the rear, turning the tide in their favour. Meanwhile, Civilis rode up to the Tungrian lines and proclaimed that he did not seek to dominate other tribes, offering to be their ally. This caused many ordinary soldiers to sheathe their swords, and two Tungrian nobles surrendered the tribe to Civilis. The *Baetasii* and Nervians soon joined as well. After the victory, Civilis marched towards *civitas Tungrorum* (modern Tongeren), the homeland of the Tungrians. The townspeople attempted to protect their city by constructing a wall, but it was ultimately sacked. This caused the support of the Tungrians, who had just surrendered to Civilis, to diminish.

Coin commemorating the surrender of the XV Primigenia legion, now at the Asmolean Museum (Oxford).

Rome's final victory and its many unknowns

This stage of the revolt is called 'The Empire Strikes Back' in several monographs/journals/websites dealing with the Batavian Rebellion. But unlike the story it refers to, in this case the Empire had the final victory and the 'rebels' seemed genuinely willing to come back into the fold.

In spring 70, Civilis was at the height of his power. However, it was evident to all that a large Roman army was likely to confront the Batavians. The leader of the new Roman military force was Quintus Petillius Cerialis, an experienced veteran, who not only had a familial tie to the new emperor

FORTISSIMI AND VALIDISSIMI: THE BATAVIAN AUXILIARIES OF THE ROMAN ARMY

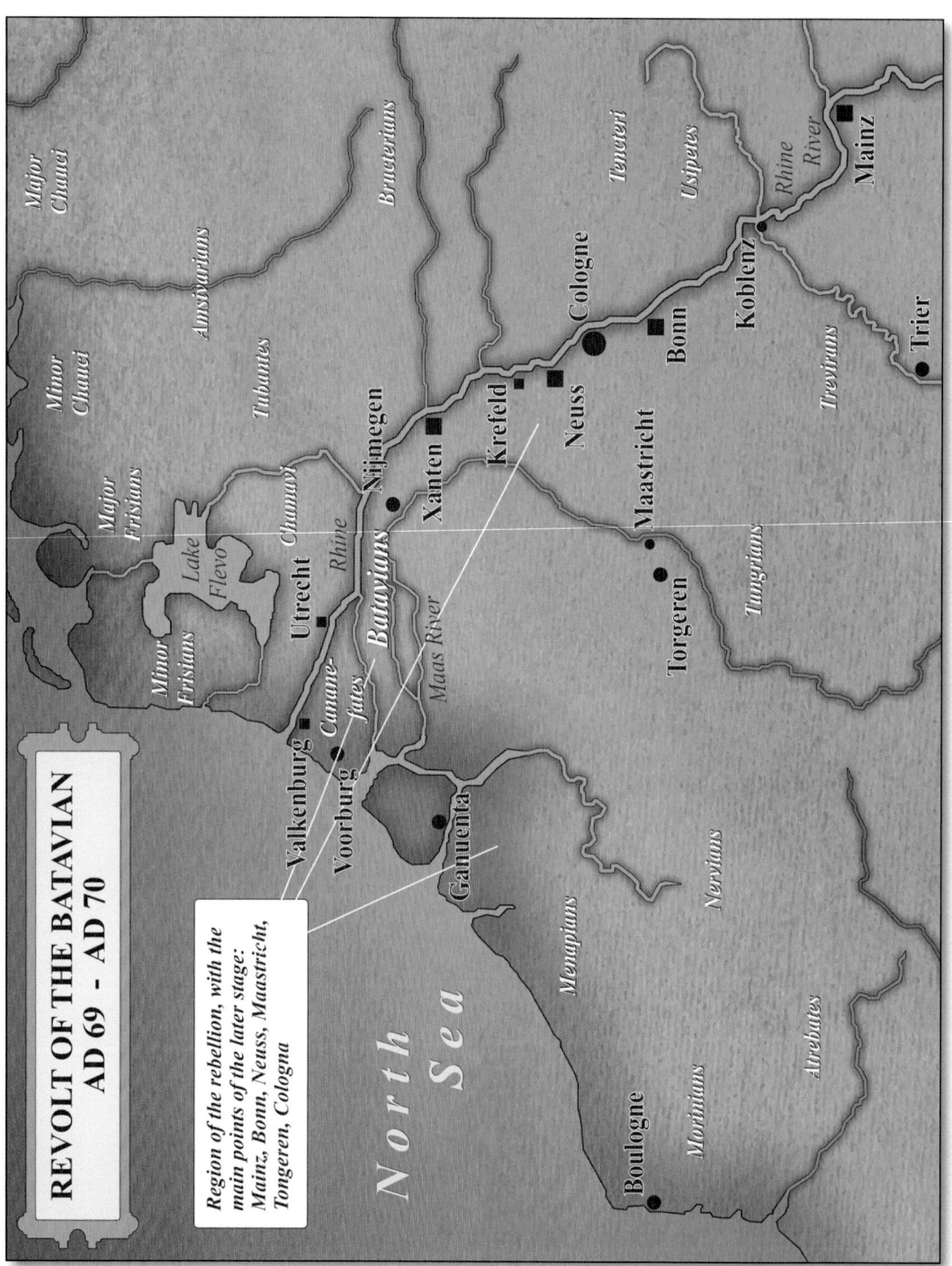

Map of the region of the rebellion, with the main points of the first stage and troops movements: Mainz, Bonn, Neuss, Maastricht, Tongeren, Cologna.

HISTORICAL TURNING POINT: THE BATAVIAN REBELLION

Vespasian but had also fought alongside him and possibly even had crossed paths with Julius Civilis during their campaign in Britannia.

The expeditionary army consisted of multiple legions that traversed the Alps via various routes. However, only three legions, namely II Adiutrix, XIII Gemina, and XXI Rapax, led by Cerialis, participated in the conflict, causing great alarm among the enemy. Before Cerialis arrived, Julius Tutor's army disintegrated as his former legionaries reverted to their original allegiance. Soldiers from the two legions that had surrendered did the same. With the enemy in disarray, Cerialis advanced to Mainz and encountered the legions IV Macedonica and XXII Primigenia in May 70. The Roman army aimed to capture Trier first, as it controlled a major road from the Mediterranean to the Rhine. Julius Civilis was occupied with chasing the guerrilla warriors of Claudius Labeo, leaving the Trevirans to face the battle alone. They tried to block Cerialis' progress near Rigodulum (now Riol) but were ultimately defeated. The following day, Cerialis entered Trier. There, he encountered the legionaries of I Germanica and XVI Gallica. He treated them kindly and showed mercy towards the Trevirans and *Lingones* as well. He only punished those who were directly guilty of treason. This kind of leaderships had been lacking in the Roman army so far in dealing with the Rhine and Gallic uprisings. Cerialis' arrival not only supplemented the force of the Roman army of the area, but inspired confidence to the men.

The Romans held the advantage in tactics, discipline, experience, and numbers. But their armies were not yet united, and this presented an opportunity for Julius Civilis and his allies. They decided to launch a surprise attack on the army at Trier during the night, possibly on the moonless night of 7–8 June, although this is uncertain. The Romans were caught off guard, and their enemies breached the camp, but the three legions ultimately managed to repel the rebels. This was the decisive battle of the war, which allowed Cerialis to start rebuilding the Rhine border and quelling the last pockets of resistance.

It was reported that Cologne had liberated itself, a development that Civilis attempted to suppress. Cerialis' three legions, potentially joined by troops from the Mainz army, rapidly marched northward. Civilis was aware that the XIV Gemina was sailing from Britannia and might land on the sandy coast of what is now Holland. He hastened back to the Island of the Batavians where he learned of one of his men's last successes: the *Cananefates* had destroyed part of the Roman navy. However, it was too late as the XIV legion had already landed and was making its way through Belgica to Cologne. The focus of the theatre of war had shifted to Germania Inferior on the Lower Rhine, and the Romans were content with this. Conquering the Island of the Batavians was not a priority, as they concentrated on pacifying reclaimed territories and fortifying the border along the Rhine. Despite this, Civilis managed to gather an army and seize control of Xanten again. Cerialis advanced against the strong forces, using XXI Rapax, II Adiutrix, the newly arrived VI Victrix, and XIV Gemina legions.

FORTISSIMI AND VALIDISSIMI: THE BATAVIAN AUXILIARIES OF THE ROMAN ARMY

The region was originally marshy, and Julius Civilis built a dam on the Rhine, causing the surrounding land to flood. This created a slippery wasteland, which was a disadvantage for the Romans. Their legionaries were burdened with heavy arms and were not good swimmers, while the Batavians and their allies were accustomed to rivers and could easily navigate the flooded terrain. The battle did not involve traditional infantry combat at close quarters. Instead, soldiers struggled in floodwaters or fought on any piece of stable ground. Archaeological evidence supports the existence of the battle, as military objects have been found in the Rhine, which has shifted its course to the location of the fight. With all difficulties, the Romans emerged victorious over the Batavians and their allies the following day, but their progress was impeded by rain. Julius Civilis' revolt came to an end when he was forced to retreat to the Island of the Batavians. The VI Victrix erected a monument to commemorate their victory, which has since been discovered.[16]

After retreating to the *insula Batavorum*, Civilis destroyed the Batavian capital at Nijmegen and the mole constructed by Drusus in 13 BC. As a result, the Waal became a much larger river, creating a formidable southern border that was difficult to cross and making it one of the widest rivers in Europe. Cerialis realised that he could not cross the river without a navy and therefore decided to wait until ships were built. After a series of minor clashes, the Batavians were able to seize the flagship of the newly built Roman flotilla in a surprise raid. However, Cerialis was not on board as he was fortuitously spending the night with a woman from Cologne. Although the Roman loss was not significant, it was still a humiliating defeat. Consequently, Cerialis decided to invade the Island of the Batavians and put a real end to the rebellion. His navy attacked the island from the west, while Cerialis crossed the Waal near Nijmegen in the southeast. Cerialis employed a well-known tactic of leaving Civilis' land and farms unharmed, while severely ravaging the lands of the Batavians. This strategy induced doubts and questions about treason. However, as summer turned into autumn, Civilis later claimed that he could have easily defeated the legions at this point, but he chose to divert the Batavians from doing so, as he cunningly surrendered a few days later.

Tacitus' narrative abruptly ends when he recounts the negotiations on a partially destroyed bridge in the Betuwe, leaving it unknown what Cerialis and Civilis discussed. However, the former alliance between Rome and the Batavians was re-established, requiring the Batavians to provide men for the *auxilia*. Despite this, the Batavians did not escape the consequences of their rebellion, as studies suggest that by this time every Batavian family had lost at least one man, and the Frisians and *Cananefates* were equally affected. Nijmegen, the capital of the Batavians, had been destroyed, and its inhabitants were forced to rebuild it downstream in a vulnerable location.

---

16 AE 1979, 413.

The fate of Julius Civilis remains unknown, but it is unlikely that he enjoyed a peaceful old age. It is possible that one of his tribe members killed him, as happened to Arminius[17] and Gannascus,[18] other Germanic leaders who once rebelled against Rome and were defeated. Alternatively, the Romans may have captured Civilis. Although Tacitus mentions that Civilis had been granted immunity, it is possible that Cerialis still broke his word to a man who had already broken several oaths. In this scenario, Civilis may have received the 'punishment of a felon' that Munius Lupercus promised him when the Batavians laid siege to Xanten: the cross.

Whatever his final fate, this was the end of the Batavian rebellion, a revolt that marked the Empire and the Batavians alike.

The new Imperial family and a shady command

In 70, the rebellion was over and we know its storyline and details mainly from Tacitus. Various archaeological and epigraphic finds support his version of the narrative; thus, we have no real reason to doubt it as a general timeline. But some other sources also come with certain additional details that could shed light on aspects obscured by Tacitus.

Sextus Julius Frontinus was the author of *Stratagemata*, a collection of stratagems written around 80. The man itself had a remarkable career under the Flavian dynasty, being a consul and governor of Britannia and Germania Inferior. His book is mainly impersonal, the only time when the author's personal involvement is mentioned being an episode from 70, at the very end of the Batavian rebellion. During the peace negotiations led by Cerialis, the *Lingones*, a tribe that had participated in the rebellion and whose territory was located between Gallia Lugdunensis and Gallia Belgica in the modern-day area of Langres, were concerned that their land would be pillaged by the approaching imperial army. Frontinus reports that Domitian commanded this army from Gallia and that the *Lingones* surrendered to Frontinus himself. The individual who would later become a writer was likely commander of a legion at the time. However, the crucial aspect of this account is that Domitian's command appears to have been 'real'.[19] The reason for our surprise is that Tacitus mentions a certain Mucianus as the commander of the Gallic armies and indicates that Domitian merely desired to have his name falsely linked to *any* triumph.

Where does the truth lie? Both writers were deeply subjective, as Tacitus' *sine ira et studio* – without hate and passion (emotional involvement) – remains a desiderate as he represented the old aristocracy that was

---

17   Tacitus, *Annales* II 88.
18   Leader of the *Chauci*, fought Roman leadership in 47 AD, during Claudius' reign, and was killed through treason and Roman plotting (Tacitus, *Annales* XI 18–19).
19   More on this in M. Dahm,'The end of the Batavian revolt. Mopping up', *Ancient warfare*, XV/2, 2022, pp. 34–39.

persecuted by emperor Domitian. Frontinus, on the other hand, wrote during Domitian's reign and seemed to benefit from it. Therefore, both writers had reasons to be dishonest, albeit in opposite directions.

To fully understand the situation, we need to establish some key details. Domitian was born in 51 and was still very young in 70. His father had recently become emperor and was known for his wisdom and prudence. The young son was considered for a command, but he wouldn't be sent to the heat of the rebellion. Instead, the more experienced Cerialis was sent there, and Domitian would need on his command an advisor with *de facto* equal powers – and that would be Mucianus. Both Vespasian and his elder son, Titus, were talented military commanders. Vespasian may have hoped that his youngest son would possess equal tactical skills. However, Domitian's reign was marked by various campaigns ranging from useless to disastrous, proving his lack of military prowess. This may have been a significant cause of his frustration, which escalated over the years, leading to cruelty and extreme unpredictability. However, the skills and weaknesses of the new emperor's young son were uncertain at the time of the Batavian rebellion.

According to Tacitus, Domitian did not actively participate in the campaigns and instead stayed in Lugdunum (Lyon). However, Frontinus reports that the *Lingones* surrendered to him, suggesting that Domitian had a formal role to play – which is not necessarily a contradiction, as surrendering is not only a matter-of-fact business, but also a symbolic act. It is unclear whether Domitian was involved in the actual battles. If he and Frontinus were attached to the II Adiutrix legion, they may have marched north with it when it joined Cerialis' army. Tacitus mentions a fabricated letter, created by Civilis, which falsely reported Vespasian's death and fell into Domitian's hands. This raises the question of whether Domitian was still with Mucianus or closer to the Batavian battlefields. Martial,[20] the famous epigraphist and Josephus,[21] the chronicler of the Jewish War, also suggest Domitian's involvement in the defeat of the Batavian rebellion. However, neither of them presents any factual evidence, but rather allusions. It is important to note that both authors wrote during the reign of Domitian and with his favour.

And although this is in theory possible, it is hard to believe that Tacitus could have hidden such a presence as the emperor's son from his history. While not completely objective, he was writing for people who had first-hand knowledge of the campaigns; this was not an ancient and half-forgotten war for his audience. Additionally, if Domitian had been with Cerialis when he overcame the rebellion, he would have mentioned it during his reign, recorded it, or immortalised it in some way. Finally, Tacitus had no reason to lie: his involvement in the defeat of this rebellion could not have washed away the sins of the future emperor, whose vanity,

---

20   artial, *Epigrammata* II.2.
21   Josephus, *Jewish War* VII. 85–88.

cruelty, and lack of political and military talents became a heavy burden for the Roman state and aristocracy over the following years.

Therefore, it is more plausible that Domitian was indeed in Gaul and that Mucianus advised him to remain there, rather than to march and join Cerialis.

What truly happened after peace was reinstalled?

The topic of local recruitment has been extensively discussed, particularly in the context of Batavian *auxilia*. This is due to the troops' unique status at the outset and subsequent changes following the 69 AD revolt. It is precisely because of the uprising that dislocations and an apparently longer lasting discomfort for the Roman leadership can be noticed in leaving the Batavian units ethnically compact and close to home. It is commonly accepted that fewer Batavians were recruited into these units, resulting in a 'denationalisation' of Batavian units by their transfer, especially in the Danube region, at the end of the 1st century. This was the generally accepted, traditional view of most historians, but the last two decades have brought new discoveries and opened the doors to new interpretations.

Upon closer examination, the situation appears to have been far more complex. A diploma from Elst dating back to 98 AD attests that a few decades after the revolt, the *ala*, which was the most powerful Batavian troop, was still stationed on the Lower Rhine. Although the unit had deserted, it was not relocated immediately.[22] It was later moved to Pannonia, where it was first recorded in 112, but the unit was moved to this area of the empire to take part in the Dacian wars or to be ready to offer support if necessary – so due to subsequent military necessity, not as a result of the rebellion.

Julius Civilis' rebellion on the Rhine drew attention to the dangers of national auxiliary troops within the Roman army, which represented tribal unities. As a result, some of the Batavian privileges were revoked, and local recruitment was replaced with mixed recruitment. Additionally, the troops were no longer exclusively commanded by local leaders. However, local recruitment continued, with only the leverage of the native Batavians among the troops being altered.[23] Recruitment from the areas where the troops were stationed was also necessary due to demographic realities. The Batavian ethnic group could not have supported recruitment perpetually and exclusively.

---

22 J.K. Haalebos, 'Traian und die Hilfstruppen am Niederrhein. Ein Militiirdiplom des Jahren 98 n. Chr. aus Elst in der Overbetuwe (Niederlande)', *Saalburg Jahrbuch*, 50, 2000, pp. 31–72.

23 J.A. van Rossum, 'The End of the Batavian Auxiliaries as 'National' Units', in L. de Light (ed.), *Roman rule and civic life: local and regional perspectives. Proceedings of the Fourth Workshop of the International Network 'Impact of Empire (Roman Empire, c. 200 B. C. - A. D. 476)', Leiden, June 25–28, 2003* (Amsterdam: Brill, 2004), pp. 116–117.

The peculiarity of the rebellion period lies not so much in the recruitment of previously underrepresented populations as in the recurrent use of emergency procedures. It is interesting to note that, in order to raise troops, Civilis and his supporters adopted methods quite similar to Roman ones, providing further evidence to relativize the 'Batavian nationalism' of this cohort prefect. Furthermore, since Civilis did not have the support of his entire people, Rome continued to recruit Batavian auxiliaries commanded by Batavian officers, particularly for the conquest of Britain, while abandoning this type of command in other auxiliary units.[24]

Despite the harshness of the rebellion and the pain it caused both sides, it is remarkable how completely and loyally the Batavians returned to the imperial army. The rebellion seems to have become a distant memory really quick. In the following chapters, we will explore the history of the Batavians after 70 AD. We will focus in particular on their role in the Roman army and the stories that were woven around these troops.

---

24 P. Cosme, 'L'impact de la guerre civile de 68-70 sur le recrutement des auxiliaires', *HIMA*, 6, 2017, pp. 83–94.

Chronology of the Rebellion

		Batavian front	Rome's throne	East
68	January			Vespasian successful in Galilee
	April	Rebellion of Galba		
	May	Julius Civilis arrested (?)		
	June		Death of Nero; Galba emperor	
	September		Galba in Rome Galba releases Civilis Execution of Paulus	
	November	Vitellius governor of Germania Inferior		
69	January	Vitellius emperor	Galba killed; Otho emperor	
	April		Vitellius defeats Otho (suicide); Vitellius emperor	
	May		Batavian units sent home	
	July		Vespasian emperor	Vespasian emperor
	August	Batavian units recalled; recruitments; Brinno revolts; defeat of Aquilius		
	September	Siege of Xanten begins		
	October	Roman counter-attack	Danube army defeats Vitellius for Vespasian	
	November			Vespasian occupies Egypt

FORTISSIMI AND VALIDISSIMI: THE BATAVIAN AUXILIARIES OF THE ROMAN ARMY

	December	Battle of Krefeld; siege of Xanten ended; murder of Flaccus; second siege of Xanten	Death of Vitellius; Vespasian sole emperor	
70	January	Proclamation of the Gallic empire		
	March	Fall of Xanten		
	May	Cerialis in Germania		
	June	Battles of Trier and Xanten		
	August	Destruction of Nijmegen		Jerusalem temple destroyed by Titus' army
	September	End of the rebellion		Fall of Jerusalem

3

The Batavians in the Roman Fold

New troops, new locations

After the revolt, the Batavian troops were reorganised.[1] However, it appears that they were still led by their own leaders, members of the tribal aristocracy and former royalty. The nine cohorts that existed before the rebellion were reorganised into four infantry troops. It is worth noting that at least two of these cohorts (the second and third, with absolute certainty) were *cohortes equitatae*, which means they also had a cavalry intervention group, and all of them became *miliariae* by the 2nd century. The *ala*, which was the elite cavalry troop, remained as it was. It is unclear how much its effectives physically changed immediately after the revolt, but it can be assumed that many of the men who deserted alongside Claudius Labeo either died, were wounded, or subsequently dismissed. The Batavian *ala* was *milliaria*, theoretically comprising 1,000 men (around 800 in practice). They were highly trained riders, often from traditional military families and prepared for a military career since childhood.

In the aftermath of the peace treaty, the cohorts returned to Britannia, where the old nine units had previously been stationed. They were documented for the first time outside the British Isle in Pannonia through a military diploma from 98 AD.[2] Cohort II took part in Domitian's Dacian campaigns and the I cohort was then transferred to northern Dacia.[3] Subsequently, the II cohort

---

1   G. Alföldy, *Die Hilfstruppen der römischen Provinz Germania Inferior* (Düsseldorf: Rheinland Verlag, 1968), pp. 47–48; J. Spaul, *Cohors²*. *The evidence for and a short history of the auxiliary infantry units of the Imperial Roman Army*, BAR International Series 841 (Oxford: Archaeopress, 2000).
2   CIL XVI 42; there is a hypothesis that the second cohort might have fought in Domitian's Dacian campaigns (in 86–87), but the evidence supporting it is quite doubtful.
3   Paul Weiss, 'Neue Diplome für Soldaten der Exercitus Dacicus', *ZPE*, 141, 2002, pp. 241–251.

FORTISSIMI AND VALIDISSIMI: THE BATAVIAN AUXILIARIES OF THE ROMAN ARMY

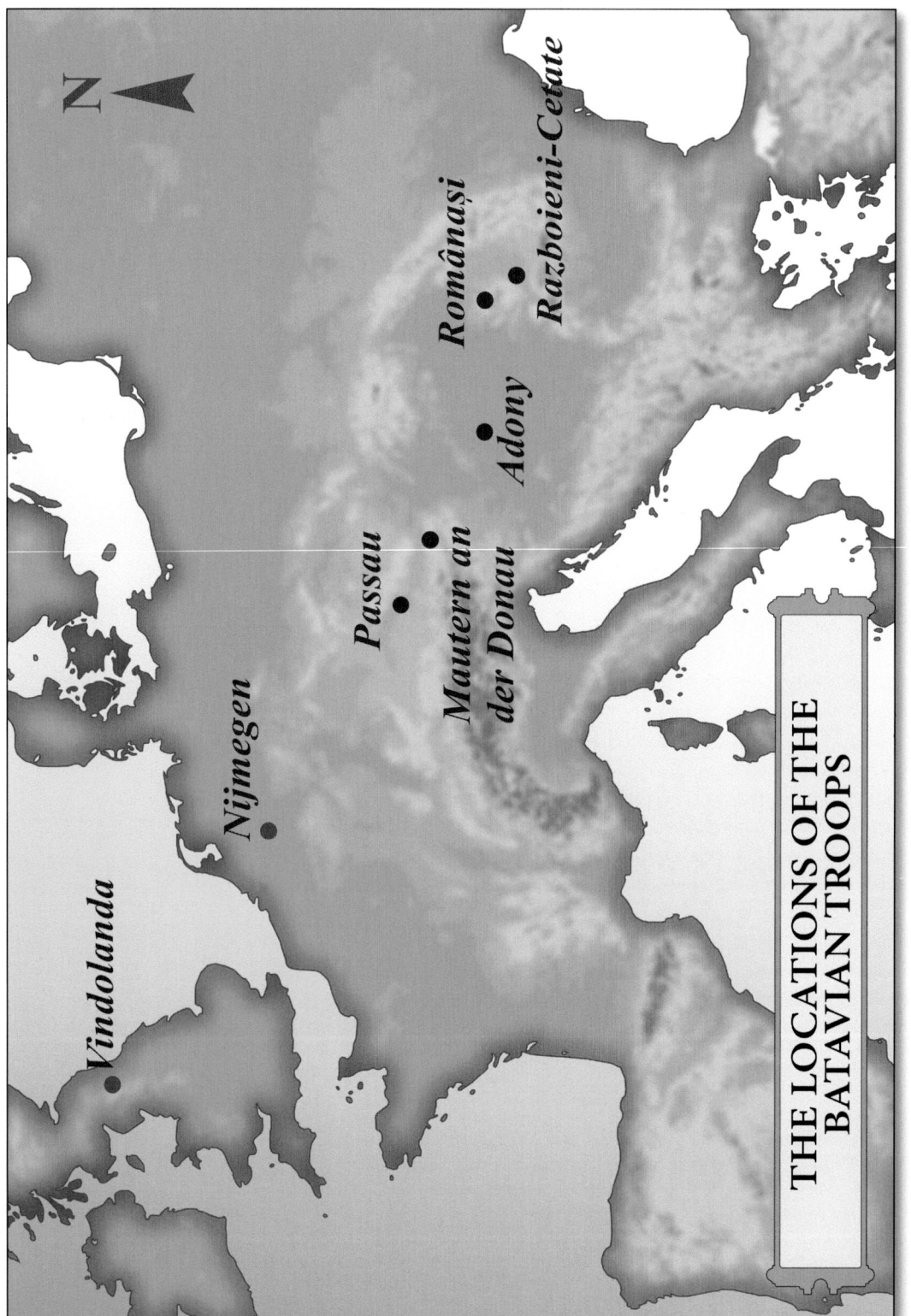

The locations of the Batavian troops

was transferred to Noricum,⁴ possible to the fort of Faviana (modern day Mautern an der Donau, in Austria).⁵ These two cohorts were collectively rewarded with full citizenship in the aftermath of the Trajanic campaign in Dacia, to which they both seem to have participated, due to their loyalty and valour.⁶ The location where the I cohort set up camp in Dacia is uncertain, but it is likely to have been Romita in northern Dacia (Dacia Porolissensis).

Cohorts III and IX were also dispatched to Britannia, and the Vindolanda tablets (to which we will get back to in the following pages) indicate that they were still present in Britannia circa 100 AD.⁷ A diploma from 107 AD attests to the presence of the III cohort in Raetia. After participating in Trajan's Dacian and Parthian wars, it was relocated to Pannonia Inferior and replaced in Raetia by the IX cohort around 135 AD.⁸ In Pannonia, it was stationed at Adony, ancient Vetus Salina, a fort just south of modern-day Budapest (and the ancient city of Aquincum). The IX appears to have had the same itinerary and settled in Raetia, at Castra Batava (the old city of Passau), right at the border of Raetia and Noricum.

During Hadrian's reign, there is an impressive vignette from Pannonia Inferior. A Batavian cavalryman named Soranus crossed the Danube in full gear in front of the emperor, shot two arrows while swimming, with the latter splitting the former mid-air. Soranus' act is documented in literary sources, namely by Cassius Dio,⁹ and commemorated by a stone monument on the Danube shore, celebrating the 'show' presented by the Batavian rider to the emperor. So, the veracity of the deed is beyond questioning. However, it is unclear whether Soranus was a member of a regular Batavian unit or the *equites singulares,* the imperial guard. Given the proximity to the emperor and the lack of any mention of a unit associated with him, it is more probable that he was part of the imperial guard, not of the *cohors* from Adony.

The history of the *ala* differs slightly from that of the cohorts. In addition to the Elst diploma, we know that in 112¹⁰ it was stationed in Pannonia Superior. It was likely also deployed here in preparation for the Dacian wars, particularly the second one (105–106). The location of the *ala* at the beginning of Hadrian's reign is unknown, but probably it was still in Pannonia. A few years into the aforementioned emperor's reign, it was deployed to Dacia. Specifically, it was stationed at Războieni-Cetate,

---

4   CIL XVI 174.
5   C. Rummel, *The fleets on the northern frontier of the Roman Empire from 1st to 3rd century* (PhD thesis: University of Nottingham, 2008).
6   B. Lorincz, *Die romischen Hilfstruppen in Pannonien wiihrend der Prinzipatszeit.* Teil I: *Die Inschriften* (Wien: Phoibos, 2001), p.145, no. 22, with references.
7   There was a historiographic discussion about VIIIth cohort attested on a single document from Vindolanda – but that would be the absolute sole attestation of the troop and we are probably dealing with a miss-spelling.
8   Lörincz, *Die romischen Hilfstruppen,* no. 305
9   Cassius Dio, *Historiae Romanae* LXIX 9.6.
10   J K. Haalebos, *Traian und die Hilfstruppen.*

located in Dacia Superior near the XIII Gemina legion from Apulum (modern Alba Iulia).

Thus, around 130, there were four Batavian cohorts stationed in different provinces, with Dacia being the only province to have two Batavian units (one cohort and the *ala milliaria*). These are the troops' last known locations, where they seemed to have stationed until the time of the military anarchy and the reorganization of the imperial army.

In the decades after the rebellion, Batavian troops were honoured for their bravery and loyalty, such as for their contribution to the Dacian wars. It is worth noting that prior to the Dacian wars, Emperor Trajan established the *equites singulares*, a unit comprising of 1,000 horsemen who were recruited from various existing *alae*. This was a more formal and institutionalised version of the Julio-Claudian and Flavian imperial guard. Unsurprisingly, a significant portion of this force was made up of Batavian horsemen.[11] The names and accompanying details on the gravestones of Batavian riders in Rome are telling, while few of them have what we would consider Germanic names, many have indications of their Batavian origin through mentions of *natione* or *domus*.[12]

Representation of the *equites singulares*, on the left, escorting the emperor in the Dacian war, from Trajan's Column.

---

11 Speidel, *Riding for Caesar*, pp. 38–55, no. 4; van Rossum, *The End of the Batavian Auxiliaries*, p. 128.

12 T. Derks, H. Teitler, "Batavi in the Roman Army of the Principate", *BJB*, 218, 2018, p. 61.

The Batavian homeland through the 2nd and 3rd centuries

> *Who would leave Asia, or Africa, or Italia for Germania,*
> *with its wild country, its inclement skies, its sullen manners and aspect,*
> *unless indeed it were his home?*[13]

Significant changes occurred in the geography of the Batavian homeland at the turn of the century. Prior to the rebellion, a *civitas* was located where the old *oppidum Batavorum* once stood, at Valkhof, and a smaller military fortification was situated on the Kops Plateau. The larger fortification at Hunerberg had been unused for some time, but following the revolt, it became the base of the victorious II Adiutrix legion. But the II Adiutrix soon departed, together with the Batavian cohorts, accompanying Cerialis to Britannia. As a result, they were replaced in the now pacified Lower Rhine area by the X Gemina legion.

Was the legion a guardian to the Batavians alone? Probably not, and perhaps not even mainly. As previously mentioned, it is likely that the Batavian aristocracy reconciled with Rome in 70 AD, and the previous treaties were renewed. These treaties were less burdensome on the tribe as a whole, at least for the time being. However, the rebellion highlighted the ongoing issues of the north-western limes.[14] The rapid rise of the Gallic Empire revealed the ambitions of the otherwise well Romanised Gallic aristocracy. This may have come as a surprise to many of the ruling groups in Rome. In addition, tribes just outside the Empire's borders, some of whom even provided Rome with auxiliary soldiers, were quick to support the rebellious Batavians. Therefore, it is likely that the legion of Nijmegen was tasked with monitoring the entire area.

The Hunerberg was a formidable structure, initially constructed of wood and timber, but rebuilt in stone around the year 90. It functioned as a legionary outpost for over 30 years. Even after it was decommissioned, its walls likely continued to leave a visual impression on passers-by and shape the surrounding landscape. Its gates influenced the routing of roads in the region for an extended period. As the legion was stationed here for a prolonged period, rather than explicitly for war as was the case in Augustus's time, the *canabae* quickly developed just outside the fort walls, separate from the main civilian settlement. These *canabae* thrived while the legion was stationed here. Archaeologically, they are notable for the *tabernae*: long strip houses that had shops and workshops oriented towards the street. After an initial phase, many of these buildings were made of stone. Subsequently, a large market and an amphitheatre were built. However, in 103/104, with

---

13   Tacitus, *Germania* 2.
14   Willems, van Enckevort, *Vlpia Noviomagus*, p. 24.

FORTISSIMI AND VALIDISSIMI: THE BATAVIAN AUXILIARIES OF THE ROMAN ARMY

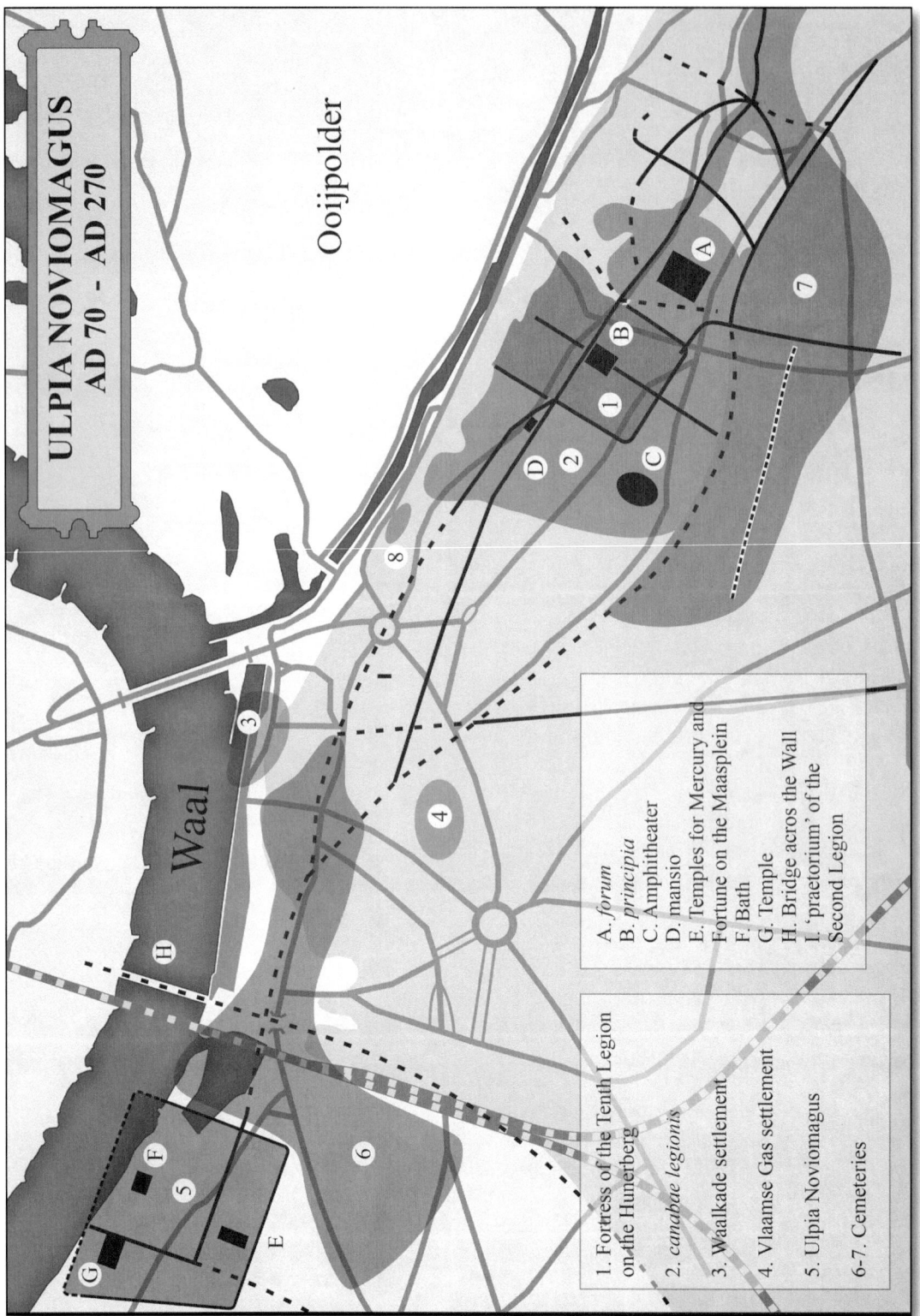

Ulpia Noviomagus.

The famous 'fast food stand' discovered in Pompei, in 2020 (photo: Luigi Spina / Pompeii Archaeological Park). Shops in the *canabae* might have been simpler in design, but we can imagine many similarities

the Rhine *limes* remaining calm for an extended period, Trajan withdrew the legion from Nijmegen and reduced the military presence in the area due to his involvement in the Dacian wars and his aspirations for a massive Parthian campaign. The *canabae* were not completely abandoned, but their heyday had passed. As they diminished in size, the town in the west gained more economic and social strength for development.

Between 82–90, a significant change occurred in the area. The frontier zone, which was previously a military district ruled by the commander of the Rhine armies, became Germania Inferior, a regular province of the Empire. The development of the local towns benefited from this change. Earlier, the civilian centre of the Batavian capital had also changed: after the revolt, the *civitas Batavorum* became Noviomagus. The name of the settlement is not attested in literary sources, but solely in epigraphic ones, unlike the *oppidum Batavorum*, which was mentioned by Tacitus and the geographer Ptolemy of Alexandria. Later in history, the settlement was referred to as Ulpia Noviomagus, implying that it had received municipal status under Trajan. This change of name must have been part of the emperor's wider reorganisation of the region. During the 2nd century, some inscription from the Empire mention Noviomagus as the 'home' of the deceased or dedicators, but Batavian auxiliaries generally still preferred to identify themselves as 'Batavus' rather than 'civis Noviomagensis'. The outlook of Batavian society may have reinforced the tendency to associate the label 'Batavian' with military virtues such as 'manliness', 'bravery', and 'loyalty'.[15] As these virtues became a source of pride, the civic affiliation was pale compared to the tribal one.

---

15 Derks, *Ethnic identity*, p. 269.

FORTISSIMI AND VALIDISSIMI: THE BATAVIAN AUXILIARIES OF THE ROMAN ARMY

For the settlement, becoming Ulpia Noviomagus represented not only a change of name, but also a slight change of location. The decision to move may have been not only administrative but also practical: the settlement was situated on the banks of the river Waal, and even minor changes in the course and flow of the river affected parts of the town and its medium-term development. It has been proven that the X Gemina was involved in the initial renovations. Most official and public buildings were now constructed using stone and after the middle of the 2nd century, the town was enclosed by walls.

Artistic reconstruction of Ulpia Noviomagus (ca. 170), painted by the artist Peter Nuyten

The main city necropolis was south of Noviomagus, but an equally large one was discovered south of the fort and the *canabae*. Some of the graves from the city cemetery were very rich, with important inventory and situated inside precincts that delimited walled gardens. The precincts could have enclosed individual property or, more often, family plots. The funerary inventory usually consists of pottery, jewels, clothing accessories, and sometimes weapons.[16] Civilian and military graves were not separated in any way, only the inventory sometimes indicating a military man. In the pottery category, very frequent in the graves of the Batavian area (from these urban necropolises, as well as the necropolises from the rural territory) are the tableware drinking sets, containing cups, beakers, jars.

In addition to the military and civilian centres of the area, it is important to consider the rural habitations that surrounded the urban point, where the majority of the Batavian population resided. The Roman dominion and presence did not significantly alter these small agrarian settlements and farms. It is worth noting that some of these locations have been eroded by the river, making archaeological investigation impossible. In the rural area, a few sanctuaries were identified, as well as the *fossa Drusiana*,[17] a channel dug by Drusus to connect the Rhine to the Ijssel river and improve the northern connection. This channel still exists today and is the reason

---

16   Willems, van Enckevort, *Vlpia Noviomagus*, pp. 138–142.
17   Tacitus, *Annales* II 8.

why the Ijssel is now a branch of the Rhine. Archaeologists have identified larger settlements emerging in the post-revolt era, indicating a population increase and a more organised urban structure. Some of the settlements served as centres for various micro-areas.

Elst, for example, a not-very-impressive *vicus* otherwise, became an important local centre due to the presence of an old sanctuary thought to have been associated with the worshipping of Hercules Magusanus, which led to its quasi-urban development. Around 100, the temple of wood is replaced by a stone one. Most probably the soldiers of the X legion from Nijmegen were involved in the reconstruction of the temple. This is the logical assumption, as the legion had stone masons and specialists in building techniques, reconstructed the fort of Nijmegen and was even involved in the extraction of the limestone from the quarry of Metz and of the tuff from Eifel.[18] But maybe more interesting than the specificities of this singular place is a pattern: around 100, major sacred places (Elst, Empel, Nijmegen-Maasplein) were reconstructed and embellished, along with minor, local sanctuaries (Cuijk). This looks like an initiative of the Roman state (through the governor of Germania Inferior), symbolising the renewed alliance with the Batavians.

The Batavian area was densely populated during the Roman era, with approximately 1,000 rural settlements registered. The increase in settlements, from early to mid-Roman periods, was of about 20 percent, which is considerable for such a short time for a pre-industrial society.[19] Trying to estimate the number of inhabitants has been a point of interest for historians,[20] with the most reasonable figures citing around 40,000 inhabitants during the early Roman era,[21] going up to around 100,000, including the rural hinterland of Nijmegen, at the turn of the 2nd century. This suggests a high population density, which put significant pressure on the arable land. Paleo-botanical analyses revealed that barley and emmer wheat were the primary crops in some of these settlements. This is unsurprising as wheat is also used to feed horses.[22] When considering the necessities of feeding the stationed troops, it is important to take into

---

18 H. Enckevort, J. Thijssen (eds.), *In de schaduw van het Noorderlicht. De Gallo-Romeinse tempel van Elst-Westeraam* (Nijmegen: Bureau Archeologie Gemeente, 2005).
19 W.J.H. Willems, *Romans and Batavians. A regional study in the Dutch Eastern Area* (PhD thesis: University of Amsterdam, 1986), pp. 394–397.
20 A lengthier discussion on this is available in I. Vossen, 'The possibilities and limitations of demographic calculations in the Batavian area', in T. Grunewald, S. Seibel (eds.), *Kontinuitat und Diskontinuitat* (Berlin: de Gruyter, 2003), pp. 414–435.
21 W.J.H. Willems, 'Romans and Batavians. A regional study in the Dutch Eastern River Area', *BROB*, 34, 1984, p. 236.
22 I. Vossen, M. Groot, 'Barley and horses: surplus and demand in the *civitas Batavorum*', in M. Driessen *et al.*(eds.), *TRAC 2008*, (Oxford: Oxbow Books, 2009), pp. 85–100.

account the limitations of the Batavian hinterland in terms of both quantity and diversity of available resources. Additionally, analyses of animal bones discovered in rural settlements have revealed a high ratio of horse bones, suggesting both internal usage and breeding for the market. It's remarkable that significant quantities of horse gear was found in almost all rural settlements, implying that horses were not only bred here, but also trained.[23]

Another element that has to be kept in mind is the presence of various fortlets and *castella* on the Rhine *limes*. Around them, *vici*, rural Roman-type settlements developed. These settlements housed the families of the military personnel, as well as artisans, merchants, and various service providers.

During this time, Noviomagus emerged as the main centre for the area, with its institutions and serving as the focal point of the area's market economy. Prior to 100 AD, the fort and *canabae* played a central role in the local society and economy, as part of a more hierarchical settlement structure than experienced in the first half of the 1st century. Ulpia Noviomagus was destroyed to never be rebuilt around 270, and the sanctuaries were also destroyed mid-3rd century, during the wars of the military anarchy period, and not rebuilt thereafter. This is the time when the Batavians exit known history.

> … and the area of Noviomagus undergoes major changes, along with the rest of Europe. The Constantinian dynasty manages to re-establish Roman control on the Lower Rhine, but this is *de iure* in nature, as the emperor doesn't have much agency and real power in the region anymore. The rural area was increasingly populated and controlled by Germanic populations. Many Frankish settlements form the period were discovered in the region, proving this shift in population structure. Nonetheless, the area was more peaceful than others at the beginning of the 5th century, as it appears that the Salian Franks protected it for the Empire – a position that mirrors that of the Batavians at their beginnings.[24] The former Batavian territories slowly became a part of Francia. In the 8th century, Charlemagne himself had a palace, in which he resided a few times, in Nijmegen – more exactly on Valkhof, the place of the ancient *oppidum Batavorum*.

***

This was the situation of the Batavian troops after the rebellion, and this was the canvas of the area from which soldiers were recruited until the end of the Principate. The following pages will focus on a few selected troops

---

23   Vossen, Groot, *Barley and horses*, p. 93.
24   Willems, van Enckevort, *Vlpia Noviomagus*, pp. 27–28.

and moments from their history. Specifically, we will present two instances in more detail: the Batavians in Britannia and the story of the *ala* in Dacia.

Tales from Britannia

The Batavians have a long history in Britannia, ever since the very start of the province. However, due to the loss of Tacitus' account of the conquest of Britannia, we must rely on scattered information and the less reliable accounts of Cassius Dio.[25] During the reign of Claudius, the south of the British main island became Britannia, a Roman province, and Camulodunum (modern-day Colchester) was established as the new power centre of the island. As previously mentioned, Batavian troops, including Civilis, played a role in the island's conquest. The Batavians' peculiar ability to swim rivers fully armed, while retaining control over their horses,[26] was demonstrated during the Claudian invasion of Britannia: in 43, the auxiliaries crossed the Medway and the Thames in the face of strong enemy opposition to form a bridgehead for Aulus Plautius' army.[27] These auxiliaries are commonly identified as Batavians.

Britannia was not pacified, however, and in 60–61 the *Iceni* revolt almost succeeded in driving the Romans from the island. Nevertheless, the rebelled Britons were defeated, most probably with the aid of Batavian troops. Tacitus describes an unusual cruelty from the Roman side at the end of the final and decisive battle,[28] where everyone, including civilians and animals, was slaughtered. Although this may be a literary device, it likely reflects the reality of the brutal conquest of Britannia.

It is relevant to note that Batavian troops were among the victorious Roman army, including the same Batavians who would rebel themselves in a few years' time. This information is important to consider in retrospect, when evaluating their commitment to the rebellion. If they had witnessed or even participated in the cruel retaliation following the Britons' rebellion, they would have had ample reason to fight to the end when the war reached their homeland. Witnessing an unusually harsh retribution may have made many of them feel that there was no turning back.

The cohorts remained in Britannia after the *Iceni* rebellion, before being recalled by Nero, in 66, in preparation for his planned campaign against the *Albani* from the Caucasus.[29] The events that followed in the years 69–71

---

25 M.W.C. Hassall, 'Batavians and the Roman Conquest of Britain', *Britannia* 1, 1970, p. 131.
26 This skill they had exhibited in the campaign of Germanicus against Arminius in attempting to cross the Ems and were later to show in crossing the Po during the civil wars of 69. Batavian cavalry could cross great rivers like the Rhine and Danube under arms and without breaking ranks.
27 Cassius Dio, *Historiae Romanae* LX 20.
28 Tacitus, *Annales* XIV 37.
29 Tacitus, *Historiae* II 27.

were presented above, as well as those leading to the restructuring of the Batavian cohorts.

Mons Graupius

As previously pointed out, following the attainment of peace, and definitely under better conditions than those experienced by the *Iceni*,[30] a portion of the Batavian troops were redeployed to Britannia.

Subsequently, in approximately 83 or 84 AD, the Batavians were engaged in a fierce battle which further reinforced their reputation. This is the point where we need to provide some information about the historian Tacitus, who was mentioned earlier as our main source for the period and one of the main creators of the Batavians' image in historiography. One of his earliest works, possibly his first, is *Agricola*, which was written in 98.[31] Agricola focuses on the life of Gnaeus Julius Agricola, a politician, general, and the historian's father-in-law. To begin with, it should be noted that *Agricola* is not entirely objective, mainly because Tacitus' admiration for the man seems to be. Agricola served as a legionary commander in Britannia in 71, during the governorship of Petilius Cerialis, who had just defeated the Batavians at that point. It is possible that some of the information Tacitus later published on the rebellion came from this source. After serving in other positions, Agricola returned to Britannia in 77 and served as governor of the province until 85. The story of these years is detailed in his son in law's work.

One of his most notable achievements was the invasion of Caledonia (Scotland), which included the Battle of Mons Graupius in 83/84. This battle was a significant military engagement between the Roman Empire and the Caledonian tribes of Scotland.[32] Although the exact location of the battle is uncertain, it is believed to have taken place somewhere in the Scottish Highlands, possibly in the area now known as Moray. The British native people used tactics of 'hit and run warfare', hiding in forests and marshes. The Batavians were perfect for this style of fighting, as they had earlier proven during the rebellion, when the legions didn't stand a chance for many months in a row.

According to Tacitus, the Roman army, commanded by Agricola, encountered a large force of Caledonian warriors led by chieftain Calgacus. This battle was an exception to the norm, as the Britons usually avoided open clashes with the Roman legions. Tacitus vividly describes the battle,

---

30 The comparison is worth making only in duet to the two rebellions' closeness in time, as the status of the pre-revolt Iceni had nothing in common to the status of the Batavians.
31 Tacitus, *De vita et moribus Iulii Agricolae*.
32 Tacitu, *Agricola* XXXVI 1. For the date see K. Strobel, 'Anmerkungen zur Geschichte der Bataverkohorten in der hohen Kaiserzeit', *ZPE*, 70, 1987, pp. 198–212.

Hadrian's Wall in the region of Crag Lough, north of Vindolanda.

highlighting the bravery and ferocity of the Caledonian warriors, as well as the discipline and military prowess of the Roman soldiers. He also provides insight into the political and cultural context of the conflict. The Roman Empire was driven by a desire for conquest and domination, while the Caledonians fought to preserve their freedom and way of life, Tacitus idealistically states. Although there is some historical debate regarding the accuracy of Tacitus' account, the Battle of Mons Graupius is widely considered a significant event in the history of Roman Britain and a pivotal moment in the ongoing conflict between the Roman Empire and the indigenous peoples of Scotland. The battle is now remembered as a symbol of the resistance of the ancient Scottish tribes against Roman expansion.

In this battle, Agrippa put his auxiliaries in the first lines, keeping the legions as back-up. Apparently, the Caledonians not only outnumbered the Roman army, but also held the higher ground. Agricola's auxiliary was focused around the four Batavian cohorts and the two Tungrian ones. The Caledonians were mowed down and trampled upon the lower inclines of the hill. Those positioned at the summit tried a manoeuvre to outflank, only to be outflanked themselves by Roman cavalry. Subsequently, the Caledonians suffered a decisive defeat, seeking refuge in the nearby woods as they were vigorously pursued by efficiently organised Roman units.

Tacitus is not prone towards graphic descriptions of battles in general, he mentions cruelty or harshness when he feels there is the case but does not detail and exemplify. But for Mons Graupius, he says that bodies and mutilated limbs were everywhere and the earth was soaking with blood.[33]

---

33 Tacitus, *Agricola* XXXVIII 94.

FORTISSIMI AND VALIDISSIMI: THE BATAVIAN AUXILIARIES OF THE ROMAN ARMY

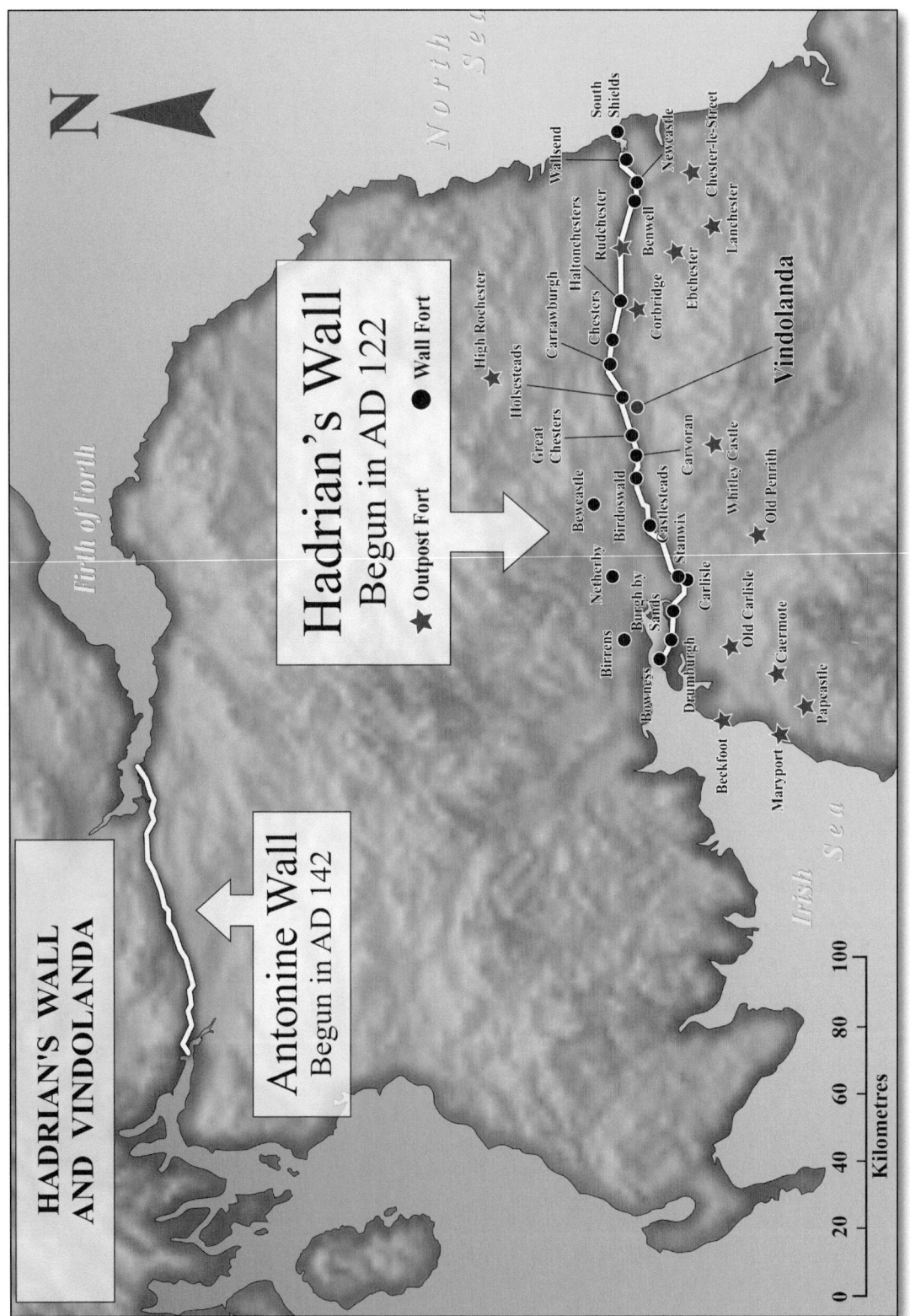

Hadrian's Wall and Vindolanda.

The image he paints is quite vivid and it basically stands for the ruthless clashing of two barbarian tribes, even if one of them was now part of the Roman army.

The Batavians lived up to their reputation and became established as one of the most important and reliable Roman troops from Britannia.

Times of peace. The Vindolanda tablets

At Mons Graupius, all four cohorts were still in Britain. Over time, they were gradually transferred, and by 90–100 AD, only two cohorts remained on the island.

These two cohorts were stationed at the Vindolanda fort, which was notorious due to its location in Northumberland, near the Scottish border – an area that posed significant security challenges for the island. The fort was constructed around 85 AD and was occupied for over 300 years. Vindolanda fort was integrated into the network of Roman forts and installations known as Hadrian's Wall, being a key location along it. In addition to its regional significance during Roman times, the Vindolanda site gained notoriety in modern days due to some of the artefacts it gave through archaeological excavations ongoing since the 1930s. The most striking and valuable feature is the preservation of documents on wax tablets, due to its swampy terrain, providing valuable insights into life in Roman Britain.

The Vindolanda tablets consist of over 400 wooden tablets dating back to the late 1st and early 2nd centuries. They are the oldest surviving examples of handwriting in Britain and provide a precious glimpse into life at Vindolanda during the Roman period. The tablets contain a variety of documents, including military correspondence, supply lists, inventories, personal letters, and even a birthday invitation. The tablets' writing is well-preserved due to the waterlogged soil at Vindolanda, which has protected the wood from decay. The tablets are thin, some only a few millimetres, and the writing is so fine that it requires a microscope or digital imaging technology to read. As examples, the tablets include a letter from a soldier named Masclus to his commanding officer requesting leave to visit his family,[34] and a letter from a woman named Claudia Severa to her friend Sulpicia Lepidina (to which we will soon return), inviting her to a birthday party.[35] Both ladies were officers' wives, proving that the high ranking personnel lived with their family. These personal letters provide rare insight into the daily lives and concerns of people living in Roman military environments. One other tablet is a report from a decurion to his commander, outlining the state of the cavalry horses under his command, others are shopping lists (which give an idea on the types of goods that were available and in demand at the fort; one tablet lists the items needed for a feast, including

---

34 *Tabulae Vindolandenses* IV 892.
35 *Tabulae Vindolandenses* II 291.

foodstuffs such as pork, cheese, and olives, as well as wine, oil, and candles), or personal correspondence (in addition to the letters from Masclus and Claudia Severa, there are many other personal letters in the collection; a letter, from a man named Aelius Brocchus to his friend Candidus includes a request for a new pair of socks and a warm cloak to be sent to him at the fort), and administrative documents (receipts, accounts, and orders; for example, one tablet is a receipt for the delivery of a load of barley, while another is an order for the construction of a new building at the fort).

The Vindolanda tablets are now housed in the British Museum in London, where they are an important resource for historians and archaeologists studying Roman Britain. They are also a popular attraction for visitors to the museum, who can see them on display and learn more about life in Britain during the Roman period. Taken together, these documents provide a rich and detailed picture, and offer insights into the daily activities, concerns, and relationships of the people who lived and worked at Vindolanda.

***

Of course, all the tablets tell fascinating stories, but regarding the Batavians, one has particular importance. Around the year 100, the *decurio* Masclus writes to the most preeminent character of the Vindolanda letters, the prefect **Flavius Cerialis**,[36] asking for instructions regarding his men's schedule.

Politely, he also asks for more beer for his troop. Masclus bears a Latin name, although a Batavian and a beer-drinker – a beverage preferred by Germans, but held in contempt by Romans and Celts alike. Local habits implanted into a Roman provincial environment go even deeper, as the

Masclus' letter to Flavius Cerialis (https://romaninscriptionsofbritain.org/inscriptions/TabVindol628)

decurio calls Cerialis *rex*.[37] Expectedly, historians debate over the exact meaning and reason for employing this unusual title lacks, but we believe that it refers to Cerialis's appurtenance to the Batavian nobility and former 'royalty'.[38] Relevant enough, the letter is addresses to Cerialis in his quality of prefect, and the appellative *rex* (*regis* textually) as part of the content, to be read by Cerialis alone. This speaks of inner relationships within the Batavian group. Once again, we must draw special attention to the Latin name, which,

---

36 *Tabulae Vindolandenses* III 628.
37 D.B. Cuff, 'The King of the Batavians: Remarks on Tab Vindol. III, 628', *Britannia*, 42, 2011, pp. 145–156.
38 Birley, *The names of the Batavians*; E. Dickey, *Latin forms of Address: from Plautus to Apuleius* (Oxford: Oxford University Press, 2002), pp. 106–107; W. Eck, 'Militärisches und ziviles Alltagsleben am Hadrianswall', *JRA* 18, 2002, pp. 666–667; A. Bowman, "Outposts of empire: Vindolanda, Egypt and the empire of Rome", *Journal of Roman Archaeology* 19, 2006, p. 87.

THE BATAVIANS IN THE ROMAN FOLD

out of context, would reveal absolutely nothing on the man's identity and background. Cerialis bears the *nomen* Flavius, so he probably was a second-generation Roman citizen. Besides the alleged 'royal' origin of Cerialis' family, we note that they didn't get citizenship from the Julio-Claudians, unlike Civilis' family. It is conceivable that his father (or family) received citizenship in the aftermath of the rebellion, as a reward for loyalty.[39] We can imagine, at this point, a dispute – or at least different views acquired as the rebellion proceeded – of two branches of the 'power elite' of the Batavians, resulting in Cerialis' group gaining power and imperial favour after Civilis' failure. With the end of the Julio-Claudian dynasty, the Batavian Julii fell from prominence as well, and the Flavii apparently became the tribe's new elite.

The tone of the letter is quite warm, the *decurio* is respectful, but the phrasing certainly implies a direct relationship between the two. Most probably Cerialis (and other Batavian commanders) were closer to their men than the normal army standards – a strength under normal circumstances, but a potential weakness if their loyalty to Rome faltered. Being close to the men didn't make Cerialis a meek commander: a different letter addressed to him by a woman asks him to *relax his severity*.[40] The woman, Valatta, was under the prefect's wife patronage, and thus was in a position to write to him directly. His wife was Sulpicia Lepidina, who belonged to one of Rome's oldest noble families. The immediate family of Sulpicia Lepidina is unknown, but the Batavian prefect definitely married into nobility and wealth. This union might also be the result of family relationships and doors opened to Cerialis' family as a result of their loyalty during (or at least at the end) of the rebellion. The *praetorium* where the two resides was archaeologically excavated and well dated. Therefore, the woman and baby shoes discovered here can be identified as belonging to Lepidina and to the couple's children.

Lepidina's slipper. (https://www.vindolanda.com/blog/the-curators-favourite-shoes)

---

39   P.A. Holder, *The Roman army in Britain* (New York: St. Martin's Press, 1982), p. 65.
40   *Tabulae Vindolandenses* II 257.

FORTISSIMI AND VALIDISSIMI: THE BATAVIAN AUXILIARIES OF THE ROMAN ARMY

One particular slipper, referred to by the curators of Vindolanda as 'Lepidina's slipper', provides a fascinating insight into her life and economic status: the shoe is both beautiful and expensive, having been imported from Gaul and bearing the stamped mark of the shoemaker, Lucius Aebutius Thales. Today, we might refer to it as a designer shoe. It was thrown away because the toe thong broke – something very easy to fix. Obviously, someone who threw away a very expensive shoe for a minor damage was someone who could easily afford those shoes. 'Severe' or not, Cerialis doesn't seem to have spared expense in ensuring his wife's comfort.

***

Getting back to the tablets, as an almost anecdotic note, we could mention that one sole letter talking about the natives and their fighting tactics. It states that they did not wear armour and had a large cavalry but did not use cavalry and weapons in the same way as the Roman soldiers. The overall image of the Vindolanda tables is one of times of peace, as it seems that the actual military work was not one of the chief preoccupations of the soldiers. However, this might be a false impression, given by the small portion from the multitude of sources which got to us, and maybe illustrating a period of relative peace in northern Britannia, which might not have been very long.

In these letters, the names often show a connection to the Lower Rhine area, but in two instances we have explicitly attested tribal appurtenance other than Batavian: a Treveran and a Vagian identify themselves as such.[41] These are also members of Germanic tribes, but what's important is that maybe they felt the need to state this identity mark exactly because they were different, because most of the other soldiers were still Batavian at the time. That the Batavian cohort attracted recruits from home even at the beginning of the 2nd century is a fact, supported by the presence of many (over 160) Batavians epigraphically identifiable.

Sometimes the Vindolanda letters give us a light-hearted feeling, but under no circumstances must we imagine that life in the fort was a vacation. Realties were tough, even in times of peace. A report for the Tungrian cohort indicates that out of the men stationed at Vindolanda, 31 were unfit for duty and 10 were suffering from eye inflammation. Excavations at the site show that the barracks were dirty, poorly lit and infested with parasites. This provided a good breeding ground for infection and disease.[42]

After 25 years of service in Britannia, what did these veterans do? Some of them stayed, for sure, as they got accustomed to the place, married local women, formed connections. But others returned home, as prove the veterans' graves, the weapons deposited in sacred placed, the continuation of the traditional military families. A proof in this direction is the presence of many late 1st century British-made brooches found on civilian sites

---

41   Birley, *The names of the Batavians*, pp. 246–247.
42   A. Goldsworthy, 'Send beer!' Life on the Roman frontier revealed by soldiers' private letters', National Geographic (online, published June 28, 2023).

around Nijmegen, which could have been brought by returning veterans of Batavian origin.[43]

The Batavian *ala* in Dacia

In 106, Trajan conquered the Dacian kingdom, making Dacia a Roman province. Afterwards, two Batavian troops were stationed in the province: the I cohort in the north, on the *limes*, and the *ala* in the central area, of the province with a strategic location. The *ala* was stationed in the modern-day village of Războieni, approximately 1.7 km north of the Mureș River, about 50 km north of Apulum (modern Alba Iulia), and 30 km down the Mureș and Arieș rivers to Potaissa (modern Turda). Apulum was the location of Dacia's first legion, the XIII Gemina, which was stationed there since the beginning of the province. Potaissa, on the other hand, hosted the V Macedonica legion from 168 onwards. The location of the *ala* provided not only mobility and prompt support for the legion (and legions, in later times) in case of need but also allowed for the control of traffic on the river and protection of the salt mines in Ocna Mureș, located 3–4 km south of the fort and identified with the ancient Salinae.

The *ala* was stationed in Dacia from 136/138, having been moved from Pannonia during Hadrian's campaign against the Iazyges in the region. It remained there until the abandonment of the province during Aurelian's reign (271–274). A thriving rural settlement developed around the fort. It is worth noting that this was a greenfield settlement, meaning it emerged and developed on its own rather than evolving from or continuing a pre-existing habitation. The ancient name of the settlement is uncertain, but an epitaph from Apamea (Syria) provides an important clue. A gravestone belonging to a military man, Aelius Verecundinus, explicitly states that he was born in Dacia, at the Batavians (*Ad Vatabos*). The settlement referred to is evidently civilian and could be linked to either the *Batavi* cohort stationed in northern Dacia or the *ala* at Războieni. Due to the greater significance of the *ala* and its adjacent settlement, Ad Vatabos is generally considered to be located here. It is worth noting the spelling with 'V' instead of 'B'. This can be interpreted as a pronunciation feature of provincial Latin, similar to the pronunciation of 'V' as 'B' in contemporary Spanish.

The site of the *ala* provided a lot of archaeological material, telling a multitude of stories which range from certain proofs of the conservation of the Batavian ethnic nucleus, to the creation of a local, specific, socio-economic environment and subsequent material culture. While the literary sources were, as we have already seen, quite consistent so far, for this sub-chapter we will mostly rely on archaeological material: various artifacts

---

43 T. Ivleva, 'British emigrants in the Roman Empire: complexities and symbols of ethnic identities', in D. Mladenovic, B. Russel, *Trac 2010* (Oxford: Oxbow Books), 2011, pp. 132–153.

which have not only functional, but also cultural meaning, as well as epigraphic texts, written on stone or pottery, which, despite their scarceness and shortness, tell comprehensive stories that allows us to unveil episodes from the *ala*'s stay in Dacia. This section will also help us dive into more details of the archaeologists' work and reconstructive methodologies – essential for the understanding of the ancient world, it's people and their inherent complexity.

So, what do we have at Războieni, the home of the *ala Batavorum* from Roman Dacia? Visible on a magnetometric prospection,[44] we have a large plan of the settlement open to interpretations. First of all, we have the *castrum*, the fort, the interior of which covers an area of about 5.2 hectares. It is a large precinct, almost double those of a normal auxiliary fort, but this comes as no surprise, as the troop was 1,000, not 500 men, plus the horses. The central components of the system have been identified: the administrative headquarters of the command (*principia*), barracks, the commander's quarters (*praetortium*) and the grain store (*horreum*). In addition, a large part of the fortification system consisting of two parallel ditches was detected.

The geomagnetic plan of the fort and settlement from the stationing place of the *ala* in Dacia.

The barracks in the *castrum* of Războieni have been especially researched, and they offered some very interesting data on how men and horses lived. It has been proved some time ago[45] that archaeologists' quest for finding

---

44 This is a non-invasive archaeological technique, which identifies buried structures based on their magnetic features.
45 C.S. Sommer, "Where did they put the horses?": Überlegungen zu Aufbau und

stand-alone stables in forts of cavalry troops was in vain, because shared accommodation for horses and men in the same building was the rule. These are the so-called 'stable-barracks' (*Stallbaracke* in German), different from infantry barracks, which have perpendicular stables at one end of the human habitations. Additional to the archaeological plans, phosphate analyses identified horse urine in soakaways placed below the stables' floor and used to collect and wash away the urine of horses. At Războieni, we have the rare privilege of a fort erected and inhabited by a sole troop, so fitted from the start to its needs. Thus, we find what we might call 'supersized stable-barracks', in which each living quarter (*contubernium*) was occupied by six men and six to eight horses.[46] In theory, the normal cavalry *contubernium* was three men and three horses, but this generalisation is partially based on old excavations and results, so maybe the Războieni 'exception' is not so exceptional and is to be identified in other cavalry forts as well in the future. The capacity of the barracks multiplied for the dimensions of the fort leads to it having hosted around 800 men and 1,000 horses – the normal effective of an *ala milliaria*.

Outside the fort, to the west, there is a cluster of buildings that were part of the village. Of course, most of the buildings in this *vicus* must have been made of easily perishable materials (wood, unburnt bricks) and on the geophysical representation we can only see those with stone foundations. Few buildings belonging to the western *vicus* can be clearly delineated and of these the most impressive is the one visible outside the fort, on its north-western corner: a 23 x 20 m building consisting of several rooms and situated about 20 m from the north-west corner of the fort. Some of the most important archaeological excavations undertaken at the site during the last few years are within this building, named Edifice I for publication purposes.

In the northern part of the area there is a high concentration of kilns, which confirms the field observations, as in that area there has always been a high density of ceramic materials, moulds, poinsons, and pottery debris. It is very likely that most of the settlement workshops were located in this area.

The structures identified in the farthest northern area are also very important. First of all, we point out the light-coloured structure in the northwest, very visible on the plan, but which does not indicate an ancient construction, but the modern gas pipe which, being metallic, perturbs the magnetometer and produces an anomaly in reading the results in the whole

---

Stärkerömischer Auxiliartruppen und deren Unterbringung in den in den Kastellen', in: W. Czysz *et al.* (eds.), *Provinzialrömische Forschungen. Festschrift für Günter Ulbert zum 65. Geburtstag* (Espelkamp: Verlag M. Leidorf, 1995).

46   A. Rubel, C. Mischka, 'Of horses and men – Garrisoning the empire: stable-barracks on a grand scale in the auxiliary fort of the ala I Batavorum milliaria at Războieni-Cetate (Alba Iulia County, Romania) and the spatial planning of Roman forts', *Journal of Roman Archaeology*, 36, 2023, pp. 96–125.

surrounding area. Also interesting are the four clusters of stone buildings visible in the far east. These are more than 130 m away from the area that has been determined with certainty to belong to the *vicus* and are most likely *villa rustica* type complexes, administering land and serving to supply agricultural products to the fort and the villagers. One of the structures is atypical in that there were at least eight ovens between the smaller buildings. There is a possibility that this complex had a craft role.

However, as mentioned above, it is possible that numerous buildings, light constructions without stone foundations, existed between those visible on the magnetometer scan. The presence of these, as indeed of all those identified non-invasively, can only be made out by intrusive archaeological investigation. What we know so far is that the *ala* created a local centre around it – production and habitation alike – prosperous enough to become an economic hub for the area. The economic development of a settlement is deeply dependent on the local society and vice versa. An agricultural production centre encourages the development of different social patterns than a commercial hub, for example. Similarly, a rural settlement based on production for consumption generates a different society than a settlement marked by a constant monetary inflow.

The economy of the site

The development of a ceramic production centre in Războieni is a highly relevant local specificity, as there was no acute need for it, the locality being close both to Apulum, where all kinds of ceramics were produced, and to Micăsasa, probably the largest ceramic production centre in Dacia, practically a workshop town. But within a few decades, the settlement of Războieni became an autonomous production centre. How do we know? We knew that there had been a production centre at Războieni since before we had the geophysical prospections, and we also knew about the kiln area, because the villagers had always recovered ceramic debris, stamps for decorating vases, and other fragments that served as indications from the area. If the existence of ceramic fragments burnt to the point of glazing and deformation could be due to local fires, the appearance of the fragments of moulds and specific tools undoubtedly indicates the existence of at least a workshop that produced good quality, decorated pottery. The first settlers from the west brought their own pottery with them, but as soon as they settled here, they resorted to imports in order to benefit from the wares they were accustomed to. The predominance of local products, however, soon took hold, even when it came to luxury vessels.

The reason for this lies in the nature of the troop and the economic situation of the soldiers in service. They were well paid, with an ordinary cavalry soldier in the ala earning 1,400 *sestertii* per year, compared to 1,200 for a legionary infantryman. Of course, officers and professional ranks were paid more. This cash flow created a fairly high level of consumption. A *sestertius* was worth a quarter of a *denarius*, meaning the approximate wage was 350 *denarii*. From 2nd century Dacia, there were preserved a number of waxed tablets from Alburnus Maior (modern day Roșia Montană) that contain commercial contracts. These tablets include numerous prices and tariffs, allowing us to determine the actual buying power of money in Dacia at the time. For example, a slave was worth between 400 and 600 *denarii*, half a house was valued at 300 *denarii*, and a piglet was worth five *denarii*. Additionally, a miner's labour for 178 days (equivalent to half a year) was valued at 70 *denarii*, plus extra meals. Thus, it can be observed that the soldiers had a high purchasing power due to their payment of a small, fixed sum for food and limited spending on entertainment while living in the barracks. As a result, theoretically, they were able to save enough money over a period of 3–4 years to purchase a slave or a house.

There was a symbiotic relationship between the troop and the specificity of the civilian settlement, the former facilitating the rapid economic growth of the latter. This relationship influenced society, created a boost to the local economy, and a desire to produce on their own. Also in the economic register, a unique discovery sheds more light on local realities. Between Edifice I and the fort we found a road, probably a secondary road, which is not visible on the geophysical plans. The road was made of layers of gravel. On this road, in an early layer of levelling, we found a gold coin – **aureus** – issued by emperor Vespasian.[47] Its value was about 25 silver *denarii*. The reverse shows a personification of Annona (the annual grain supply), seated on a throne, holding a sack of grain and some ears of grain in her hand. Soldiers received part of their payment in gold, which most probably they used for keeping/saving, but carrying such a coin in one's purse is quite unusual, indicating the intention of a large purchase, or transporting money to a safe place. There were no banks in the ancient world, so money could be stored with an authority (soldiers had a troop treasury office, where they generally kept their savings), or at a private location (family house, friends' locations, etc.). We don't know who lost the Vespasianus *aureus*, if he was military or civilian, or why he was carrying such a large sum upon himself at the time, but we can surely assume that he greatly regretted the loss. Concluding, this coin speaks, most of all and beyond a personal story, about the general layout and state of mind of the settlement: a place where somebody can lose a high value of money on a road in construction, regardless of circumstances, is a place with an above the average cash inflow and implicit standard of living.

Staying in the realm of material culture, **pottery**, the most frequent find of the archaeologist on the dig, has the capability of indicating patterns of consumption, cultural influences and even cultural affinities, for all layers of society. In our settlement, western influence certainly exists, and we can

---

47   C. Gazdac, G. Bounegru, R. Varga, 'Paying and saving in Gold in The Roman Army. The Aureus of Vespasian from Războieni-Cetate and the evidence of Gold Coins in Roman Dacia (Romania)', *Journal of Ancient History and Archaeology*, 7/2, 2020, pp. 94–102.

still be fairly certain of the existence of a Batavian core of the elite unit, supplemented by local recruits. Some vessel types suggest consumption patterns linked to the military area or even links to the Rhine area. Such is the case of a biconical cup found at the site, which has no analogues in other Dacian assemblages, but does have analogues in northern Gaul (Gallia Belgica), one of the main areas from which the Batavians imported pottery.

Terra sigillata (Samian ware, a luxury red pottery with elaborate representations on it)[48] is always an indicator of local wealth and a source of knowledge – on economic ties, trade, markets, etc. – for the historian. The artefacts from Războieni did not reveal a large concentration of imported *terra sigillata but* instead show pre-eminence of local products. The majority of imported fragments is dated to 135–160 AD, originating from Lezoux in Central Gaul and clearly being associated with the first 'wave' of Batavians who arrived in Dacia, during the settling of the troop and its following civilians at Războieni. The workshops from Lezoux were very 'posh' during the first three quarters of the 2nd century AD, imports from them being present within the whole Empire. Later on, the settlement developed its own production centre, hence replicating its own version of *terra sigillata*. This suggests a high demand on the local market, understandable in the context of the presence of the *ala*, explained above.

But some of the most spectacular ceramic imported artefacts discovered at Războieni are two **anthropomorphic vessels**.[49] One of them is very fragmentary, with only the right eye of the human figure preserved, while the other is largely intact and has an interesting feature: two phallic representations, one on the back of the vessel and one on the left cheek of the human figure. The earliest anthropomorphic continental Roman vases were found on the Rhine-Raetian border, exclusively as part of the Rhenish legionary repertoire of the first half of the 1st century AD. Their distribution extends as far as the Upper Danube and the Low Countries, which is also the homeland of the Batavian troops; most anthropomorphic vessels come from Cologne, Colchester and Nijmegen. In Roman times, they continued to be used in burial rituals, but this function became adjacent to everyday use: in domestic altars, where sacrifices were offered daily in the name of a tutelary deity.

The pots are very relevant in the context of evaluating the culture of the settlement we have under scrutiny. Beautiful and 'peculiar' imports such as these, reflect cultural roots and at the same time shaped mentalities. The larger of the two vessels has no traces of usage (burning on the inside or the outside) and was discovered in a waste pit, so thrown away by its owners,

---

48 Britannica, T. Editors of Encyclopaedia. "terra sigillata ware." Encyclopedia Britannica, March 24, 2011. https://www.britannica.com/art/terra-sigillata-ware.
49 G. Bounegru, R. Varga, 'Two face pots from the vicus of Războieni-Cetate (Alba County)', in S. Nemeti, E. Beu-Dachin, I. Nemeti, D. Dana (eds.), *The Roman provinces. Mechanisms of integration* (Cluj-Napoca: Mega Publishing House, 2020), pp. 221–232.

not destroyed along a building. A hypothesis that comes to mind is that somebody from the troop or immediate family, coming from the Batavian homeland to Dacia, brought the anthropomorphic urn in order to use it for funerary purposes. But the artefact broke before being used and it ended up in the waste pit of the house they lived in – for us to find.

Short note on a stray helmet

The military inventory recovered from the site of the *ala* is not spectacular, consisting of generic artefacts, what one would expect to find in the context of a Roman cavalry troop. As we will see into more details in the following chapter, the equipment of the Roman auxiliaries doesn't conserve specific elements or weapons of choice, being rather standardised and undifferentiated at the scale of the Empire.

The anthropomorphic vessel with phallic symbols from Războieni-Cetate.

But one artefact pertaining to the military equipment category, discovered in the area of Războieni draws attention. It is a bronze cavalry helmet, a piece of defensive equipment that can be typologically defined and thus we can draw certain conclusions based on it. Unfortunately, it is an out of context discovery from the 19th century, coming from a local's backyard,[50] in a village situated approximately four kilometres east from the site of the *ala* (modern day Lunca Mureșului; there was no Roman settlement ever identified here, so it is very complicated to assume how and when the helmet got to be buried at the location of its modern discovery).

The helmet pertains to the so-called Guisborough type (named after the place of the first discovery of this model of head piece, in the UK). It has a vertical forehead plate decorated with snake-like motives (typical, with certain variations, for these helmets), and a narrow neck guard. Inside the neck plate it has the number XVIIII inscribed backwards, probably nominating the sub-unit (*turma*) to which its owner had belonged. A 500-men *ala* had 16 *turmae*, while a *milliaria* had 24[51] – belonging to the 18th

---

50 Tg., 'Római sisak Székely-Kocsárdról', Archaeologiai Értesítő, 1888, pp. 184–185; J. Garbsch, *Römische Paraderüstungen* (München: Beck's, 1978), p. 100.
51 A. Goldsworthy, *The complete Roman army* (London: Thames & Hudson, 2003),

unit automatically describes the owner of our helmet as member of an *ala miliaria*. The *turma* might have been more important than the name of the owner himself in a certain regard. A helmet from Rijswijk has the marks of two (consecutive) owners, both belonging to the same *centuria*.[52] There are indications that the troop sometimes bought pieces of equipment from new veterans and kept them as patrimony. Probably the sub-unit could buy them itself and then re-sell it to its own recruits.

Interesting enough, this type of helmet becomes regular for auxiliary cavalry troops around 100, afterwards developing certain variants.[53] During the second century, masks were also attached to these helmets. So, the dating corresponds with the stationing of the *ala* in Dacia. But what makes it even more associable with the *ala* and not with one of the legions of the area is its typological attribution by J. Nicolay to auxiliary cavalry alone.[54] We must indicate that his study is concerned with the Batavian armament from the Lower Rhine area, so there is a possibility that certain variations and mutations took place in the provinces. But given all this data, the geographical place of the discovery, the typology, the number of the sub-unit, the highest chance is that the helmet belonged to a Batavian from the *ala*.

What's in a name?[55]

Last but not least, we have some written materials, epigraphic sources, which tell the story of some of the people from the *ala*, or associated with it. The texts are generally scarce, with little information, thus we must make use of everything there is.

Often in epigraphic texts, the name and very little else is all that we get on the mentioned people. Onomastics, the science of studying people's names, can give us important details about the identity and even the lives of people in the past. Names reveal social and cultural details about the person who bears them and their family. Also, for the Roman Empire, names can indicate a person's legal status, i.e. whether he or she was a citizen of the Roman state enjoying full political and economic rights, a peregrine (thus lacking citizenship, but still being part of the Roman system), an ex-slave (*libertus*), or a slave.

---

pp. 57–58.

52 P. van der Heijden, A. Koster, *Romeinse helmen in Nederland* (Leiden: Hazenberg Archeologie, 2017), p. 10.

53 J. Nicolay, *Armed Batavians. Use and significance of weaponry and horse gear from non-military contexts in the Rhine Delta (50 BC to AD 450)* (Amsterdam: Amsterdam University Press, 2007), p. 15.

54 *Idem*.

55 The syntagma comes from Shakespeare's *Romeo and Juliet*, where the young woman muses, related to the lovers' 'family names and the families' rivalry, that a name is just an exterior label and the essence of things is all that matters.

It should also be noted once again that the Batavians' onomastics is Latin par excellence, having lost its Germanic component before entering Latin written sources, as we already mentioned in the first chapter. Thus, we have the great disadvantage of not being able to search for names whose etymology can be linked to a tribal or at least geographical origin, but only to interpret and contextualise Latin names. In order to show what data onomastics can reveal about the becoming of the *ala* during its stay in Dacia, we will examine three samples of epigraphs, in chronological order.

Some of the most intriguing names from the *ala Batavorum* come from *instrumenta* (inscriptions written on various objects, not carved in stone). More exactly, we present a few fragmentary plates bearing *graffiti* which were discovered in the barracks.[56] The texts from the plates are written in Latin, were incised *post cocturum* (after the pots were fired, so basically scratched on the vessels) and are to be dated during the *ala*'s first years in Dacia. The shards record names, obviously the owners' names, in genitive or nominative, as eating and cooking vessels were stored in common within the barrack. The names could be read when the bowls were placed with the rim downside, indicating how they were put on the shelf in the barrack. The writing itself is a combination of cursive and capital letters, basically reflecting the style of the soldiers' handwriting, as well as the necessities of scribbling on rough clay. Literacy was widespread among the troops and everybody could write their name on a plate and read those of the others. The names are fragmentary, but their reconstructions are Celsus, Dionysius and Capito. Besides the Latin, very common, names, one notices the presence of an etymologically Greek one – Dionysius. This is a very important addition to the onomastics of the site. Greek names became a tradition in Batavian military families, after the northern recruits from the Flavian Imperial Guard employed them[57] and they later on became a mark of family military tradition. So, one of our men might actually be part of a Batavian military family, with a father or grandfather serving in the imperial guard.

These apparently modest *graffiti* are important for more than one reason. First, we know, by name, three men that were serving in the *ala Batavorum* at the same time and shared a barrack. To have even more insight into their lives, we have the texts written by their own hands, on a personal object. Why inscribe the bowls? Because they did not want them mixed, of course. This gives us the idea that they had a basic hygiene notion that made them not want to share their plates with each other and consider them strictly personal belongings.

Another man attested at Războieni, later on in time then the barrack-mates, and who most likely did not serve in the *ala* (since we assume that military status would have been recorded as a distinction of pride), is Flavius

---

56   R. Varga, A. Rubel, G. Bounegru, 'Pottery vessels with *graffiti* discovered in the fort of *ala I Batavorum* in Dacia', *Electrum,* 2024, pp. 127-141.
57   Birley, *The names of the Batavians*; van Driel-Murray, *Ethic soldiers*, p. 201.

FORTISSIMI AND VALIDISSIMI: THE BATAVIAN AUXILIARIES OF THE ROMAN ARMY

Hadrianus. This inscription is particularly interesting because we find it on a 3rd century AD dedication to Hercules Magusanus. Unfortunately, the text doesn't give us more, but what is relevant is that the deity, the main god of the Batavians, was still worshipped by the Batavians from Dacia at that point in time.

The last individual attested from the troop is one of its commanders, Marcus Publicianus Rhenus, who dedicated two votive altars in the middle of the 3rd century AD.[58] The inscriptions are both relatively deteriorated, but they have been recently re-read and reconsidered. The RTI visualisations[59] of these inscriptions revealed the name of the prefect with absolute certainty. The personal name, Rhenus, is not a toponymic name, indicating an origin in and of itself, but it rather appears to be a theonym, instead, referencing the deity of the river Rhine – Rhenus. This conclusion is suggested by other instances of the name and comparable forms: they do not denominate specifically people from the various provinces, the second generation of a family 'from the Rhine' (as it is usually the case of toponymic names) but are instead used to designate people living in the Rhine area. The name honours the river in its divine quality – as all rivers, especially the major ones, had a divine incarnation in the Roman religious imaginary.

The altar of Marcus Publicianus Rhenus, discovered in the legionary fort of Potaissa and now preserved at the History Museum from Turda

---

58 S. Nemeti, R. Varga, D. Deac, 'A vignette from Dacia under Philippus Arabs: revisiting the altars of Marcus Publicianus Rhenus', *Chiron,* 2024, pp. 429-448.

59 Reflectance Transformation Imaging (RTI) is a new imaging technique that creates hyper-realistic digital surrogates that are interactively controlled by the viewer. This new method is based upon the synthesis of multiple digital images of a subject in a fixed position collected from a fixed camera position (source: https://mci.si.edu/reflectance-transformation-imaging).

THE BATAVIANS IN THE ROMAN FOLD

A most interesting attestation of the name Rhenus is to be found in Vindolanda: the name Rhenus features in two personal letters, although it is difficult to say whether they refer to the same person or not, as we are dealing with two very fragmentary documents. One is addressed by a certain Rhenus, slave of Similis,[60] to his friend Primigenius,[61] while the other sends greetings from an unknown man to Rhenus and other individuals.[62] Other than the case from Dacia, these instances of Rhenus, or Rheni, are the only points of connection between the name and Batavian realities.

The name of the prefect suggests once again that there was still a connection between the Low Rhine area and the Batavian troops from the provinces at this late stage of their existence. A nucleus of soldiers – elite soldiers, with very specific cavalry skills – appears to have been recruited from the Low Rhine regions, with Rhenus, the troop's commander, being part of this old Batavian military elite.

***

The Batavian troops remained well respected after the rebellion, being an important part of the Roman army in its imperial 'classical' form. As the military anarchy began, we slowly lost track of the Batavians – as well as of the most auxiliary troops of the Empire. The Roman army was reformed and reorganised, the migrations became more of a reality and the whole world in which the Roman Empire had to subsist changed.

What we see in the becoming of the Batavian troops is a tribe of traditional soldiers who turned professional soldiers, respected and trusted, even after a huge rebellion. While the Batavian militaries adhered fully to their martial identity, keeping loyal to commanders recruited from their own tribe, the Batavian home became increasingly populated, with Ulpia Noviomagus claiming the role of the most important city of the northern border of Germania Inferior.

---

60   As an anecdotal side point, this man might be Flavius Similis, one of Flavius Cerialis' correspondents.
61   *Tabulae Vindolandenses* 2347.
62   *Tabulae Vindolandenses* 3657.

4

Military Equipment and Fighting Technique

This chapter focuses on a number of important aspects of Batavian identity within the Roman army: what did their military dress look like, how did they fight, how were they used on the battlefield? While the Roman army was generally fairly uniform in terms of weaponry, armour and fighting style, there were particularities for certain troops at certain times, as well as developments and changes. In the case of auxiliary troops, the characteristics of the original population that formed the troop and its fighting style were often retained as much as possible but also adapted to fit into the normal tactics of the Roman army. Similarly, once integrated into the imperial army, equipment could retain some specific features, as it was the case of the Iberian slingers. However, these pre-Roman features remained more distinguishable for infantry troops. Cavalry fighting required more or less the same set of skills and generally the same type of equipment. Of course, there was a difference in appearance between the Moorish and Batavian cavalrymen, for example, but the European *alae* as a whole had strong similarities in equipment, fighting style and general aspect.

The presentation of the Batavians' fighting style and armour will be useful in understanding their place in the Roman army, the impact they had on the places they were transferred to during their history and perhaps help us understand how their transgressions were forgiven and forgotten.

The Equipment

The equipment of a soldier, Roman or not, consists of defensive and offensive weapons and some other functional/decorative elements (e.g. belts). For the ancient military, the defensive weapons were a form of armour (leather or metal-made), helmet and shield. Among these elements, the helmets are the most spectacular in the case of the Batavians. As well as providing protection, a helmet is an expression of status and impresses opponents. The offensive weapons are swords, spears and daggers.

MILITARY EQUIPMENT AND FIGHTING TECHNIQUE

At the beginning of their contacts with Rome, the Germanic warriors were well clad, but often without armour. As offensive weapons, they had axes, swords and spears. The swords were *spatha-type*, longswords, resembling those of the Celts. Some sources consider that these populations' swords were the inspiration for the Roman cavalry *spathae*. Their shields were painted, but probably not in a regular manner as the Romans', but according to the owner's taste and superstition. Helmets, when worn, also varied in design. As time went on, more body armour was employed, leather or metal, in the style of both *lorica squamata* (scales) and *lorica hamata* (chainmail). They were both flexible and adjustable to horse-riding, although the scales offered a better protection from arrows, especially in the areas where it was doubled, such as the shoulders. But horsemen are not particularly vulnerable in those parts, and scales can be shattered by upward thrusts – which is the more common blow when one is on horseback. Thus, the *lorica hamata* was generally preferred by cavalry soldiers in the Roman army.

Before being integrated into the Roman army, most Batavian warriors had a shield and a light spear (so basic defensive and offensive weaponry), and only 30 percent, according to archaeological finds and reconstructions, also possessed a sword. The more complex equipment seems to have been used by cavalrymen, the elite group of the Batavian army.[1] As a consequence of the transformation of these former tribal troops into regular *auxilia*, some equipment similar to the legionaries' made its way into their inventory. The main evidence comes from the weapons found in early Roman graves, particularly in the Middle Rhine area. The meaning of the funerary inventory is confirmed by numerous finds in 1st century auxiliary camps of weapons traditionally regarded as characteristic to the legions, such as plate cuirass, *gladii* and *pila* (spears).[2]

The main swords used by infantry soldiers were typically the double-edged *gladius*. Daggers (*pugiones*) were employed as complementary weapons. When encountered on a battlefield, they signalled the presence of infantry, whether legionary or auxiliary. Cavalrymen were usually equipped, as we have seen, with the longer *spatha*. While on horseback, they could use it as a slashing weapon, whereas the *gladius* was primarily a stabbing weapon.

Under the metal armour, soldiers wore cloth: a short tunic, trousers, a scarf protecting the neck and sock-like covers for the feet. The *gladius* and *spatha* were attached to a belt worn at the waist, or a baldric worn over the shoulder. Leather 'aprons', decorated with small metallic plaques hung from the front of the waist belt. They were supposed to keep the hem of the tunic down, as well as to serve as decorum. The typical footwear was the *caliga*, an open-toed sandal. In colder climates, the *caliga* was replaced by more solid,

---

1   M. Zerjadtke, 'Germanic warriors and amphibious warfare. No barrier to battle', *Ancient warfare*, XV/2, 2022, pp. 26–33.
2   J. Nicolay, *Armed Batavians*, p. 61.

boot-like footwear. As for the horses, they were equipped in a manner very similar to modern equestrian equipment. The saddle was made of leather, but did not have stirrups, which did not become common in Europe until the 6th and 7th centuries. The bridle and reins were held together by a piece of metal, sometimes decorated. In battle, a chafron was worn to protect the face, eyes and head. Models and decorations varied. In general, Roman horses wore no armour, at most a thick cloth covering the body in battle or when exposed to harsh environmental conditions.

Germanic shields were typically made of light wood. Spearheads were relatively short and light, weighing between 70 and 120 grams; some of them had fire-hardened tips, and others were made of horn. Warriors carried a maximum of four kilograms of equipment, or six if they also had a sword and the adjacent paraphernalia. The largest part of this weight consisted of metal weapons, while the rest mainly comprised items made from dry wood. This made it easy to carry the weapons while swimming without difficulty. Subsequently, in the Roman *auxilia*, the Batavians generally fought wearing a chainmail *lorica*, a helmet (sometimes with the scalp imitating hair, and sometimes with a facemask, as we will see), using a *spatha* and an oval shield. Nonetheless, we saw that the river-crossing skills evolved, and the Batavians were able to swim fully clad even after adopting the Roman-style equipment with equal proficiency.

Arms and armour have been discovered by archaeologists in a variety of contexts, both civil and military, but probably the most spectacular and best preserved finds come from sacred deposits in sanctuaries and rivers. The latter were common to both Germanic and Celtic populations, and of course the deposits didn't only consist of weapons, but also included all sorts of household objects, jewellery, sacred dedications, etc. A well-known site is Kessel/Lith, where many weapons have been found in the river.[3] They seem to have been deposited there whole, but obviously many had deteriorated over time. As well as typical local, Iron Age – tradition long swords and scabbards, Roman artefacts have also been found: two *spathae*, a *gladius* and a *gladius* sheath fragment. All date from the 1st century AD, indicating that the custom of depositing weapons at Kessel continued into the early Roman period. Spearheads were also discovered, some pre-Roman, some Roman. A few pieces of equipment found at Kessel/Lith seem to be specific and to have disappeared by the end of the 1st century: e.g. swords have a hilt with bronze circlets, a feature that is not preserved for the inventory of the Batavian cohorts and was not to be discovered in Britannia or Dacia.

An enormous quantity of material, dating back to the stone age, has been discovered in the Waal river at Nijmegen. The military inventory is of about 80 objects, mainly dating from post-rebellion periods. The weaponry consists of 12 helmets, a plate armour component, a shield boss and three swords. Other probably sacred deposits of weapons found in rivers are to be associated with washed-out forts, such as Corvinum at Lobith (the Oude

---

3   Roymans, *Ethnic identity*, p. 108.

MILITARY EQUIPMENT AND FIGHTING TECHNIQUE

Waald is the local river), or the Angeren – 'Loowaard/Kandia' site (in a cut-loop of the Rhine).[4]

Sacred deposits were also laid in temples and sanctuaries. At the temple of Empel, over 200 fragments of weapons and military equipment were discovered, along with horse gear. They were probably votive deposits, most likely dedicated to Hercules Magusanus, which had undergone some form of 'ritual destruction', as evidenced by the deliberate damage to many of the weapons.[5]

But soldiers didn't always deposit their personal weapons when their military service was over. Possessing Roman weapons and equestrian equipment and perhaps displaying them in their homes, would also have given their owners prestige in the local community to which the veterans returned or settled. This was particularly true in the earlier recruitment periods when the items were considered exclusive and unique. Helmets, armours, swords were often personal *memorabilia*, items hard to part with. Some veterans kept certain pieces of arms and equipment and left them as part of their inheritable assets; some were gifted to sons (or other close family members) who joined the army and some became grave goods. In other instances, as ownership inscriptions prove, weapons were simply sold to other soldiers or new recruits, or to a military troop which then sold them to one of its members.

The most spectacular pieces of Batavian military equipment are the **helmets**. Cavalry helmets from the Lower Rhine area became a historiographic and visual landmark, as they are present in every type of description of the area in ancient times. In the following paragraphs we will describe some of the most interesting and specific helmets, noting that they represent only a minority of the total number of finds.

Masks in the shape of stylised classical faces were affixed during the 'classical era' to helmets, giving rise to masked helmets. An iron mask, often covered with bronze sheets was attached to the helmet. Of course, the visual impact was tremendous, as a mask hides fatigue or fear and is intimidating, especially when used by a large group. Arrian's manual on cavalry tactics, written in 136,[6] links the masked helmet primarily to ceremonial cavalry equipment. As a result, many helmets were dubbed as sports helmets by their initial discoverers but are now considered to have been used in battle. While the vulnerable bronze masked helmets were mainly for parades, the heavier iron examples could also be used in actual combat. One of the most famous masks from Nijmegen, a symbol of the town itself (see the following chapter), is an iron mask covered with silver-plated bronze and partly gilded. The forehead plate is decorated with human busts and the whole design is very elegant and visually beautiful. Nevertheless, this artefact gives us another indication of the use of these helmets in real war. Analysis showed

---

4   J. Nicolay, *Armed Batavians*, pp. 125–128.
5   Nicolay, *Armed Batavians*, pp. 120–124.
6   Arrianus, *Ars tactica*.

FORTISSIMI AND VALIDISSIMI: THE BATAVIAN AUXILIARIES OF THE ROMAN ARMY

The Nijmegen masked helmet. It was discovered in 1915, on the sandy bank of the Waal. It is now stored at the Valkhot Museum, in Nijmegen.

that it was made of more layers of metal and when a 1:1 replica was shot with a *ballista* (a Roman crossbow), it proved to resist the impact very well.[7] It would have offered real protection to the wearer, very much in the style of medieval cavalry helmets, which also covered to rider's entire face.

The discovery of masks, in terms of contexts and quantity, supports the assertion about their utility in combat, as also evidenced by a specimen from Kalkriese, found at the site of the Teutoburg Forest battlefield. It's important to note that helmets with masks share technological similarities with other helmets, using the same materials and manufacturing methods. They prove to be equally effective and qualified for combat, despite their luxurious appearance and ornate bells. The increasing popularity of these helmets in the early 2nd century further supports their use in battle. Helmets with masks became valuable additions to the protective armour of both the cavalry and heavy infantry of the Roman army.[8]

Archaeological discoveries from the Kops Plateau in Nijmegen indicate that the helmet bowls were sometimes covered with actual fur or human and animal hair. In the case of the Kops Plateau helmets, the applications turned out to be made of horsehair. This organic cover consisted of braided ribbons combined with circular bands around the head. On account of their find contexts these helmets with remarkable organic decorations can be dated to the Claudio-Neronian period. But similar artefacts, cavalry helmets with 'hair' have been discovered in other parts of the Low Rhine area as well, one other known example coming from Xanten.[9] Two of these helmets bore dotted marks on the cheeks, under the eyes. They were called 'tattoos', but we do not know if Batavians had the practice of tattooing their skin in reality, nor do we have sources on it.

In the 2nd century, helmets were characterised by a long, steep nape, a broad and sloping neck plate, and large curved cheek pieces that protected both the chin and cheeks. One must note that the cheek piece also protected the ears, as noise must have been unimaginable when riding in a full metal armour, but the cavalrymen wearing these helmets also couldn't hear

---

7   Heijden, Koster, *Romeinse helmen*, p. 13.
8   K. Narloch, 'The cold face of battle – some remarks on the function of roman helmets with face masks', *Archäologisches Korrespondenzblatt*, 42, 2002, p. 381.
9   M.J.M. Zandstra, *Miles away from home. Material culture as a guide to the composition and deployment of the Roman army in the Lower Rhine area during the 1st century AD* (Nijmegen: Radbound Universiteit, 2019), p. 224.

MILITARY EQUIPMENT AND FIGHTING TECHNIQUE

The Kops Plateau helmets with the bowls covered with animal hair.

anything. They must have known in advance very well what to do, as well as to where and when to look for orders transmitted through signs and signals. This is an important detail for understanding the unity of the troops and their ability to quickly coordinate and adapt to battlefield situations.

In addition to their practical use, the helmets of the Batavian cavalry were also a sign of status. The helmets often bear owner marks (the name of the owner inscribed with punctuated, *graffiti*-like marks). In some cases, several owners are listed, giving us a history of the ownership of the piece. It's worth noting that the helmets, especially the decorated, masked ones, sometimes unique in detail, were not cheap. Investing in them is a sign of status – and the desire to 'show off' that status – and ritually depositing them is a sign of both wealth and piety. Just as they were willing to spend to enhance their status and make themselves fearsome in battle, they were equally willing not to recoup their investment and to settle the final score with their military past by demonstrating their deep piety.

A final question is who produced the weapons. The legions, as well as the *auxilia*, had a quite large number of men responsible of producing and repairing weapons, so they were mainly self-sufficient as units. This is evidenced by the numerous traces of metalworking from army camps, consisting in moulds, production waste, miscast and discarded pieces. At Kops Plateau, large quantities of bronze slag and scrap prove that the army was metal working during the 1st century AD.[10] The same situation

---

10 J. Oldenstein, 'Zur Buntmetallverarbeitung in den Kastellen am obergermanischen und rätischen Limes', *Bulletin des Musees Royaux d'art et d'histoire*, 6, 1974, pp. 192–193, 195.

FORTISSIMI AND VALIDISSIMI: THE BATAVIAN AUXILIARIES OF THE ROMAN ARMY

Helmet from Mainz with the name of two successive owners, Titus Allienus Martialis and Statorius Tertius, both from the *centuria* of Antonius Fronto. (photo: https://www.karwansaraypublishers.com/blogs/ancient-warfare-blog/the-imperial-gallic-i-helmet)

is registered in the legionary fortress of Hunerberg.[11] Nevertheless, there was still a need for imports, even if the scales tipped and the majority of imported weapons were replaced over time by a majority of locally produced weapons. We can even see a decline in the quality of daggers when the Lower Rhine armies stopped importing them from northern Italy and started producing them locally.[12] For the 2nd and 3rd centuries, we also have archaeological records of private workshops developing in the *canabae* and the villages of the area. Some of these civilian artisans could have been ex-soldiers who had worked in the *fabricate* of the troops and after becoming veterans decided to put their skills to good use in private businesses.

In conclusion, the weapons and equipment of the Batavians were the regular *militaria* of the Roman auxiliaries. They were adapted to the type of troop (cavalry or infantry) and to the general fighting style of the Roman army. The cavalry helmets, the most spectacular pieces of Batavian military clothing, speak of fighting style (troop unity and responsiveness to orders, as well as visual impact), but also of expression of status and piety, as the most beautiful helmets that have come down to us are from ritual depositions.

Fighting skills

We have already discussed the Batavians' fighting prowess and their fame as 'amphibious' troops, as these qualities are an integral part of their history within the Empire, of what made them valuable for Rome, and thus respected. This ability seems to have been specific to several tribes of Germania Magna, as we see Arminius' men crossing rivers and swamps

---

11   B. van Daele,'The military fabricae in Germania Inferior from Augustus to A.D. 260/270', *JRMES*, 10, 1999, p. 127.
12   Nicolay, *Armed Batavians*, p. 132.

MILITARY EQUIPMENT AND FIGHTING TECHNIQUE

with equal aplomb, surprising Germanicus' army. However, the Batavians were the one tribe to be integrated into the Roman army and to 'appropriate' this particular skill.

Below we will look at some of the instances where we know the Batavian troops fought and then draw some conclusions. While the Germanic troops in general became well integrated within the Roman army, they still retained peculiarities, mainly during the 1st century. Tacitus tells the story of the *Sugambri*, a tribe neighbour with the Batavians, who sang and struck their weapons against each other while fighting the rebellious Thracians in 26. It's worth noting that the *Sugambri*, unlike the Batavians, had a Celtic genetic legacy, but the long-term geographical proximity imprinted many common features on the cultures and behaviours of both tribes. In 69, when the 'Germanic cohorts' attacked Placentia,[13] they sang fiercely and bare-chested, clapped shields and stepped to the rhythm of the *barritus*, a traditional Germanic pre-fight intimidation tactic.[14]

So, once again, what do we know so far about the Batavians as soldiers of the Empire? They were traditional cavalrymen, very adept at river crossing, fierce and probably feared. They were often employed as advanced skirmishers and mostly as shock troops. Their reputation was surely built on the image created and which they created for themselves in Rome, as the population of the capital saw the emperor's guard more or less on a regular basis and certainly more frequently than they saw the Batavian auxiliaries (which was never, for most of Rome's inhabitants). If Caesar did indeed have Batavian guards, or Germanic guards from the area and population mix soon to be identified as 'Batavian', it is not surprising that they were already established as feared and loyal warriors by the time of Augustus.

As far as we know, the Batavians were mainly used as a shock force, surprising the enemy and acting as the spearhead of the rest of the army. Chariovalda crossed the river where it was allegedly impossible to do so, surprising the *Cherusci* and enabling Drusus to win. If the troops which crossed the Medway and the Thames during the conquest of Britannia were indeed Batavian, and at least a part of them was, they were again the spearheads of the Roman army, landing an unexpected blow to the enemy. At Mons Gaupius, they were used for fighting in an impossible position – outnumber and on the lower ground – and again they helped Rome's army gain victory. For the Dacian war, Batavian troops were brought in Pannonia, at the Dacian kingdom's frontier, but we don't have accounts of how they were used in the conflict. The *ala* certainly wasn't brought in Dacia for the war – and this takes us to one of the most puzzling realities of the Batavian troops: the *ala*, the most respected, most impressive, best paid, one of the 6 *alae milliariae* of the Empire, is not explicitly attested to have fought in the major wars of the 1st – 3rd centuries. With one almost ironic exception: the Batavian rebellion,

---

13 Tacitus, Historiae II 22.
14 M.P. Speidel, *Ancient Germanic warriors* (London, New York: Routledge, 2004), p. 115.

when indeed it fought up to the standards, especially under the leadership of Claudius Labeo. But then it fought against the Roman legions, not alongside them. We constantly find the *ala* in the Nijmegen or the Lower Rhine area and have no attestations of it participating in Rome's wars. After being moved to the east, it doesn't fight in the Dacian war. Why? The explanation may lie in the presence of another shock cavalry force on the Dacian battlefield. The *Mauri* cavalry played a huge role in the downfall of the Dacian capital, and they were commanded at the time by a very popular figure, Lusius Quietus, trusted by Trajan and part of his inner circle. Perhaps their unavoidable presence made it unnecessary to have another elite cavalry troop, which would have played the same role of a special force. Maybe it fought against the *Iazyges* under Hadrian, maybe it fought against the *Marcomani* under Marcus Aurelius, when they invaded Dacia. But even before this, it must have fought along the Roman army at some point, after its organisation as a regular troop. The point is that their skills were like a certainty, almost axiomatic, and much of their effectiveness must have been based on renown. Probably the troop – and not only it, but all Batavian troops – made a point of demonstrating their strength and skill in smaller conflicts, border skirmishes, in order to keep their reputation beyond doubt and the aura intact.

We now see the Batavian soldiers as visually impressive, used as some sort of shock troops, even though they were part of the regular army.

The Batavian 'brand'

Who were the Batavians? Objectively, hard to say. But we can say for sure that in the eyes of the Romans, the Batavians had a strong 'brand'. They brought to life all the qualities and wild nature of the Germanic tribes but loyally put in the service of Rome and its emperors.[15]

They were the 'headliners' of the northern auxiliaries because they were formidable, but even more, because they were wildly willing to integrate and they seemed to like, perpetuate and eventually help construct the image that the Romans created for them. The Batavian material culture, besides its unavoidable specificities, is to its core Roman provincial material culture, their weapons are Roman, and even their names are Roman. In our opinion, the quick and swift Latinisation of the names is the most vivid proof that the Batavians not only wanted to get integrated into the Empire, but took pleasure from it, found their place within its fabric. Hercules Magusanus, the god whose pre-Roman roots we do not know, survived because a god is more important than worldly things and because Rome was prone to adopting the conquered peoples' gods. In time, adding to the initial integration process, the Batavians auxiliaries acquired Roman tastes and once returned home, introduced these elements to the local society.[16]

---

15 van Driel-Murray, *Ethnic Soldiers*.
16 S. Heeren, 'The material culture of of small rural settlements in the Batavian

Given the veterans' large numbers and their monetary affluence, their tastes and preferences weighted a lot for the patterns of local culture development.

Due to this perfect integration, to this day, what defined and constructed Batavian identity is difficult to pin down. Nonetheless, we must remember that shared practices, pledges, songs,[17] anthems and such are all invisible and all extremely strong in defining a community – especially a martial one. The Batavian identity in the imperial era was a combination of projected identity and adopted identity, as the Batavians seemed to have been willing to exhibit the features that the Romans projected upon them. Long postings, such as the ones from Britannia and Dacia, surely had an impact on the troops, as the local recruitment from the same pool influenced the troops composition and identity. But, as we have seen in the previous chapters, we have reasons to believe that a Batavian nucleus was preserved. This makes sense because it conserved the troops' identity, core skills, visual impact and connection to the commanding officers – as the presence of Rhenus from Dacia, so late in the history of the Principate, proves.

The border, the *limes* of Germania, separated two lifestyles, a 'Romanized' and a 'native' one. As anywhere and anytime the border is a mosaic and, in this puzzle, the *Batavi* are the military settlers who embrace Romanisation and all that it brought. Their fate, as professional soldiers, was intertwined with that of the Empire. Their loyalty was that of a maybe once marginalized group who gained respect and recognition under the Roman state.

---

area: a case study on discrepant experience, Creolisation, Romanisation or Globalisation?', in H. Platts *et al.* (eds.), *TRAC 2013: Proceedings of the Twenty-Third Annual Theoretical Roman Archaeology Conference, King's College, London 2013* (Oxford: Oxbow Books, 2014).

17 Speidel, *Ancient Germanic*, pp. 62, 97–100.

5

The Batavians Rediscovered

The following pages will outline the rediscovery of the Batavians, who, like many ancient 'barbarian' populations, faded into obscurity during Late Antiquity and the Middle Ages.

Tacitus, along with many other classical writers, was the main and primary source of information on the Batavians and was himself rediscovered during the 16th century. The Netherlandish humanists were impressed by the discovery of these eminent ancestors in his writings. Erasmus of Rotterdam, the renowned religious reformer, referred to his countrymen as 'Batavians'. Due to the popularity of his works, this quickly became an essential element in defining a Dutch individual identity.

In 1572, the religiously reformed Netherlands rebelled against Emperor Phillip II of Spain, thus initiating the Eight Years' War. As with any rebellion against a powerful empire, identity constructs were crucial for the morale of the rebels. The rediscovery of the Batavians, their alleged independence and might within the Empire, served exactly the narrative that troops and civilians needed. In the early 17th century, the Batavians became the subject of popular history, literature, and theatre. In 1609, Petrus Scriverius wrote *Batavica illustrata*, a history of the Batavians. Other writers, such as the poet Theodore Rodenburgh, followed suit with works like *De trouwen Batavier* (1609) and *Batavierse vrijagie-spel* (1616). Although these titles are now obscure, they were popular in their time and contributed to the Batavians' importance in Dutch identity. It is important to note that while these works may have had literary value, their historical depictions were largely fictional.[1]

Pieter Hooft's *Baeto*, published in 1617, is a play of historical significance.[2] Hooft drew a direct descent of the Dutch in the 17th century

---

1   I. Schöffer, 'The Batavian myth during the sixteenth and seventeenth centuries, in J.S. Bromley, E.H. Kossmann (eds)., *Britain and the Netherlands* V. *Some political mythologies. Papers delivered to the fifth Anglo-Dutch Historical Conference* (The Hague: Nijhoff, 1975), pp. 78–101.
2   E.O.G. Haitsma Mulier, 'Grotius, Hooft and the writing of Dutch history in the

and Tacitus' Batavians. The play's protagonist, an early Batavian leader named Baeto, ultimately accepts adhering to a form of royal rule, which caused controversy among the mainly republican Dutch elite.

The Batavian myth was considered a political asset, worth displaying for the young republic. In 1619, the Dutch East India Company named the capital of Java, modern-day Jakarta, Batavia. The name was changed only after World War II, when the island proclaimed its independence.

Batavians, particularly Civilis, were a popular subject for painters, including Rembrandt, who was commissioned to create a painting for the Amsterdam Town Hall. He chose the scene where the Batavians swore in a grove to rebel and fight the Romans. Civilis, dubbed Claudius instead of Julius, wears a lush crown and 17th century clothing, but more importantly, he has a severed eye. This was based on a remark of Tacitus,[3] who said that Civilis passed himself as a second Sertorius[4] or Hannibal,[5] whose disfigurement he shared; the Carthaginian general lost vision in an eye due to infection. The painting was briefly exhibited in the Town Hall before being removed, mainly because of the blind-eye representation, and is now displayed at the Nationalmuseum of Stockholm.[6]

Rembrandt's *The conspiracy of Claudius Civilis* (*De samenzwering van de Bataven onder Claudius Civilis*).

Dutch Republic', in A.C. Duke, C.A. Tamse (eds.), *Clio's mirror. Historiography in Britain and The Netherlands* (Zutphen: De Walburg Pers, 1985), pp. 55–72.
3   Tacitus, *Historiae* XIII 3.
4   Quintus Sertorius was a Roman aristocrat who rebelled against the Senate and tried to establish an independent kingdom in the Iberian Peninsula (80–72). He was flamboyant and a very good general but was eventually defeated by Pompey the Great and assassinated.
5   General who commanded Carthage's army against Rome during the Second Punic War (218–201 BC). He is famous for crossing the Alps into Italy with his war elephants and for crushing the Roman armies at Cannae. He was finally defeated by Scipio Africanus at Zama but remained in the Roman collective memory as one of the Republic's most formidable adversaries.
6   M.D. Carroll, 'Civic ideology and its subversion: Rembrandt`s "Oath of Claudius Civilis"', *Art History*, 9, 1986, pp. 12–35.

FORTISSIMI AND VALIDISSIMI: THE BATAVIAN AUXILIARIES OF THE ROMAN ARMY

In the 19th century, the Batavians were idealistic republicans fighting against a greedy empire. However, this narrative conveniently ignored the Dutch state's own colonial empire and the Batavians' integration as soldiers of the Roman Empire. In 1813, the Netherlands became a kingdom. However, the ruling principles and the Batavian founding myth remained equally important. The most prominent book of the period, which influenced what and how the Batavians were taught in schools, was Jan Wagenaar's *Vaderlandsche Historie Verkort*, written in 1782.[7]

But at the end of the 19th century, the image of the Batavians, though still very Romanticised, started to gain accuracy from correlation to archaeological finds, a certain degree of understanding in interpreting those finds. Thus, H.D.J. Van Schevichaven, said:

> The Roman antiquities from the Netherlands show that the masters of the world did not live there with the same splendour and luxury as they did in neighbouring Gaul, Britain and the Rhine area. No colonies were founded on the poor heathlands and moors; no high rank official brought the magnificence and richness from the south. Remains of splendid villae, mosaic floors, marble cornices, columns and images have not been found here.
>
> *The Batavian territory, too poor to produce tributes and taxes, was left to its own devices. But the sons of this unruly soil, hardened by the continuous struggle with an ungrateful nature and unfavourable climate, were fit for military service. Thus, the Batavian territory was considered a breeding ground for soldiers of the Roman army.*[8]

During the first half of the 20th century, the narrative didn't change much. A more radical version was proposed by national-socialist authors such as P. Felix, who has Civilis, in his play *Claudius Civilis*, side with Arminius and unify their fights against the Empire.

The ways in which the Batavians were rediscovered, then used to build up a national identity is not by far an exception in Europe. Equal process took place for the Gauls, the Celts, the Dacians and so on. This was a stage of discovering individuality beyond the Roman unifying narrative.

Civilis was a notable figure, but his story is relatively short and typical, making it difficult to create a legend comparable to those of other barbarian leaders who defied Rome. There are more paintings and engravings representing Civilis, besides the Rembrandt painting, but they are mainly unaccomplished artistically and obscure nowadays. One statue, a fantasy

---

7   For more bibliography and an interactive approach on 'The Batavian' myth, see: https://www.ucl.ac.uk/dutchstudies/an/SP_LINKS_UCL_POPUP/SPs_english/batavian_myth/index.html.

8   H.D.J. Van Schevichaven, *Epigraphie der Bataafsche krijgslieden in de Romeinsche legers, gevolgd van een lijst van alle geregelde hulptroepen tijdens het Keizerrijk* (Leiden: Bij A.E. Sijthoff, 1881), i–ii. Translated by Derks, *Ethnic identity*, p. 239.

in itself, is in Tervuren and was sculpted by Lodewijk Van Geel, in 1821–1822. It was commissioned by the Crown Prince Willem Frederik of Orange and it was to embellish the gardens of his hunting pavilion. The statue is a classical 19th century nude, resembling more a Homeric hero than a Batavian warrior. Another statue, unimpressive again, but worth mentioning due to its location, is Civilis' representation from the Town Hall of Nijmegen. A generic representation, without any visual hints that we are looking at a Batavian/Germanic warrior, the statue now displayed is a recreation by Albert Termote, made in the 1950s, after the 16th century original was destroyed during World War II.

The stories of others who rebelled against Rome led to the creation of 19th century visual landmarks that became part of European popular culture. Arminius was not only the leader who troubled Augustus' last years, but we also know his life story after the Teutoburg Forest, his resilience in continuously fighting the Empire, and his eventual downfall at the hands of his own men. The *Hermannsdenkmal* marks the area of the infamous battle. Boudicca, like Civilis, was a historical figure for only a few years, but the strength of her story as Britain's warrior queen is undeniable, as well as the fascination it still exerts. The bronze *Boadicea* statuary group is located near the Westminster bridge, in one of London's busiest areas. And finally, Vercingetorix, the Gaulish chieftain, benefitted from the most imposing adversary and chronicler at the same time: Caesar, Rome's best tactician of all its history. His *Vercingetorix* monument stands at Alesia, the site of his near victory over Caesar.

Civilis, who might have been just as accomplished a leader as these three, did not have the same memorable elements in his story. He did not haunt an emperor's dreams (as far as we know), did not lead a rebellion that almost caused Rome to lose an entire island, all while being a queen, not a king, nor was his showdown with Caesar, but rather with the almost forgotten Cerialis.

The second half of the 20th century didn't bring a Batavian Asterix to the public, but after 1945, the study of the Batavians became more and more scientific and less ideological, following the developments of European historiography and archaeology. As well, this ancient population began to be known to a wider public with a bit more accuracy than during the 19th century. All research and archaeological discoveries led us to the knowledge we now hold, as presented and synthetised in this book.

Civilis' statue from Tervuren.

But even as approaches get more scientific, the Batavians are part of a reconstructed collective identity. In 2020, the city of Nijmegen installed on the banks of the river Waal a huge statue representing the Nijmegen helmet. The monument, work of the artist Andreas Hetfeld,[9] is almost six metres tall, 2,000 kilos, and is fittingly called *The face of Nijmegen*. The statue has become the symbol of the city in the few years passed since its disclosure, and the association with the Batavian past and lore seems to be beneficial.

The face of Nijmegen.

In 2021, a new Roman-era sanctuary was discovered at Herwen-Hemeling in the Netherlands. The sanctuary revealed several temples and a significant number of dedications, most of which were made by officers of the Roman army. Although other deities are attested, Hercules Magusanus holds preponderance as the 'official' god of the Batavians since their earliest historical stages. The press release stated: *Never before has such a complete complex been found in the Netherlands with a temple building, votive stones and pits with the remains of sacrifices. In addition, the amount of limestone sculpture fragments is unprecedented*,[10] proving that each day can bring us closer to a better and fuller understanding of the Batavians and their history.

---

9   https://www.hetfeld.nl/.
10 https://www.heritagedaily.com/2022/06/roman-sanctuary-discovered-in-the-netherlands/143933.

Appendix I

Glossary

Most of the terms in this glossary have already been explained in the book, but we thought it would be useful to reprise them in the form of a small dictionary. We have chosen to translate the words, when possible, but some of them have no proper equivalent in English, so they have been kept in Latin. They are marked with italics.

Ala	auxiliary troop in the Roman army, representing a cavalry unit; it could consist of 500 or 1,000 (*ala milliaria*) soldiers;
Artefact	any object that is manufactured or modified by man;
Canabae	civilian settlement in the immediate vicinity of a fort; it has no administrative autonomy because the land is under military jurisdiction;
Castrum (fort)	military fortification, surrounded by walls of earth and timber or stone, inside which were the barracks where the soldiers of a troop lived, the commander's quarters, the command building, barns, baths, sacred spaces, etc.;
Cohort	auxiliary troop in the Roman army, representing an infantry unit; it could consist of 500 or 1,000 (*cohors milliaria*) men;
Consul	one of the two highest magistrates in the Roman state; in the republican period they represented the executive power (later taken over by the emperor) and were elected for a one-year term; in the imperial period the office became honorary;
Decurion	a) municipal: member of the municipal senate, which exists in every Roman city; b) military: officer commanding a sub-unit of 10 men;
Demography	the science that deals with the statistical study of the human population, especially in quantitative terms;
Equites singulares Augusti	guard of the emperor; moral successor of the Julio-Claudian and Flavian guard, created by Trajan; formed of elite riders and stationed in Rome;
Epigraphy	the science that studies inscriptions;
Freedman (*liberus*)	former slave, who earned his freedom during his lifetime; although a citizen, because of servile birth, he could not run for public office;

FORTISSIMI AND VALIDISSIMI: THE BATAVIAN AUXILIARIES OF THE ROMAN ARMY

Germani corporis custode	the guards of the first emperors, considered personal guards, unlike the official praetorian guards (and more difficult to buy off or bribe, as they were foreigners, less enthralled by the political games of the capital);
Gladius	short, two-edged sword;
Instrumentum	an instrument, tool, and other artefact intended for ordinary and domestic use;
Legate	envoy of the emperor, usually as provincial governor (*legatus Augusti*); commander of a legion;
Legion	the largest and most important unit of the Roman army, of around 5,000 men; heavy infantry, accompanied by a small cavalry force;
Limes	a term describing the Roman frontier line and adjacent fortification systems; it is a modern term, as the Romans didn't have the concept of 'border' in the same manner as contemporary societies do;
Lorica	body armour; the most frequent types were *hamata* (chain mail), *segmentata* (cuirass of metal plates), *squamata* (metal scales) and *musculata* (anatomical cuirass);
Marcomanni	Germanic tribe which, in alliance with the *Quasi* and other peoples, attacked the Roman Empire and waged a destabilising war between 166–181;
Militaria	the collective term for equipment used by the military for offensive and defensive purposes;
Military diploma	a document inscribed in bronze certifying that the holder has honourably completed service in the army (25 years under normal conditions);
Peregrine	a person who was not a Roman citizen; he could, however, be a citizen of the city/town of origin, with quite broad rights;
Pilum	spear or javelin, about two metres long;
Praetor	the second magistrate after the consul in the Roman state, in pre-imperial times part of the executive power; as with consuls, there were two praetors simultaneously, elected for one year;
Praetorium	the headquarters or residence of a Roman official, governor or military commander;
Spatha	straight, long sword;
Thermae	public baths, usually large, designed for relaxation and social activities; bathhouses were similar but smaller-scale public or private facilities;
Tria nomina	the naming system of Roman citizens, consisting of: *praenomen* (personal name), *nomen* or *nomen gentilicium* (name of the gens – family, clan) and cognomen (nickname, became hereditary and distinguished branches of a *gens*);
Tribe	(original) administrative unit which included Roman citizens;
Turma	a cavalry sub-unit;
Vicus	village: could be administratively dependent on a city or have autonomy;
Villa rustica	a rural property comprising the owner's dwelling and outbuildings, which had a use dependent on the main type of activity that the farm was developing (sheds, warehouses, stables, etc.); often located at the centre of a large agricultural estate (*latifundium*).

Appendix II

Roman Monetary System

Since we have referred to prices and wages in a few instances in the book, the following is a summary of the Roman monetary system, with its main coins, as they were in the period of the Principate.

1 *as* = small coin, primary unit of measure
2 asses = 1 *dupondius*
4 asses = 1 *sestertius*

16 *aces* = 1 *denarius*
8 *dupondii* = 1 *denarius*
4 *sestertii* = 1 *denarius*

2 *denarii* = 1 *antoninianus*
25 *denarii* = 1 *aureus*

As	copper coin of very low value; by the middle of the 3rd century, it was almost out of use;
Dupondius	copper coin, worth two *asses*; in reality, however, it never weighed as much as two asses;
Sestertius	bronze coin (in the Republican period it was issued in silver), widely used in the 2nd century; like the *as*, it also lost its value and use in the mid-3rd century;
Denarius	silver coin, very commonly mentioned in written sources; over time, it lost its real value, becoming only 50 precent silver (in the period of Septimius Severus);
Antoninianus	silver coin first issued by Caracalla (M. Aurelius Antoninus Caracalla – hence the name); individualising, it depicts the emperor with a crown with rays; it had from the beginning a low silver content (40 percent), but, despite devaluation, it circulated until the age of Constantine the Great (307–337);
Aureus	the standard gold coin of the Roman Empire; it was used for saving, being too valuable for everyday use; it retained its high gold concentration and was only replaced by Constantine with the *solidus*, which weighed less.

Appendix III

List of Roman Emperors

The history of the Roman Empire is divided into three main periods: the Regal period (625–510 BC), the Republic (510–31 BC) and the Empire (31 BC–476).

The Imperial period, the one we are mostly focusing on in this book, is further divided into Principate and Dominate. The Principate begins with the assumption of imperial power by Octavian Augustus and ends with the reign of Diocletian (284–305). It is also Diocletian who divides the Empire into East (Eastern) and West (Western) – the end of the Dominate and the Roman Empire is in 476, when Rome was conquered by Germanic tribes. The Eastern Empire continues to exist as the Byzantine Empire until the 15th century.

For Batavian history, however, the Dominate is no longer relevant. The chronology here presents the succession of emperors during the Principate period.

Julio-Claudian dynasty
Augustus (31 BC–14)
Tiberius (14–37)
Caligula (37–41)
Claudius (41–54)
Nero (54–68)

Year of the Four Emperors
Galba (68–69)
Otho (69)
Vitellius (69)

Flavian dynasty
Vespasian (69–79)
Titus (79–81)
Domitian (81–96)

LIST OF ROMAN EMPERORS

Antonine dynasty
Nerva (96–98)
Trajan (98–117)
Hadrian (117–138)
Antoninus Pius (138–161)
Marcus Aurelius (161–180)
Lucius Verus (161–169)
Commodus (177–192)

Year of the Five Emperors
Publius Helvius Pertinax (193)
Marcus Didius Severus Julianus (193)
Pescennius Niger (193)
Clodius Albinus (193)

Severan dynasty
Septimius Severus (193–211)
Caracalla (198–217)
Publius Septimius Geta (209–211)
Macrinus (217–218)
Elagabalus (218–222)
Severus Alexander (222–235)

Military anarchy/Crisis of the Third Century
Maximinus (235–238)
Gordian I (238)
Gordian II (238)
Pupienus Maximus (238)
Balbinus (238)
Gordian III (238–244)
Philipus Arabs (244–249)
Decius (249–251)
Hostilianus (251)
Gallus (251–253)
Aemilianus (253)
Valerianus (253–260)
Gallienus (253–268)
Claudius II Gothicus (268–270)
Quintillus (270)
Aurelianus (270–275)
Tacitus (275–276)
Florianus (276)
Probus (276–282)
Carus (282–283)
Numerian (283–284)
Carinus (283–285)

Appendix IV

Short Biographies of the Ancient Authors Mentioned in the Book

Ancient sources describing episodes directly related to the history of the Batavians are, as we have already seen, not extremely numerous. Throughout this text, however, we mention several ancient authors with their often indirect but equally valuable contributions to our knowledge.

We believe that the reader would benefit from some brief biographical medallions, in order to understand more easily who the people are we are referring to and to whose works we refer to. The authors are presented below in alphabetical order.

Lucius Flavius **Arrianus**: ca. 89–146/160; Roman historian of Greek descent, form Nicomedia. Coming from the local Greek aristocracy, he had philosophical and historical preoccupations, his best known writing being *The Anabasis of Alexander*. Around 125 he became friends with the emperor Hadrian, who appointed him to the Senate. Afterwards, he became consul and governor of Cappadocia for six years.

Caius Julius **Caesar**: 100 – 44 BC; Roman general and statesman. His career marks the passing from Republic to Imperial rule. He was a member of the First Triumvirate along Crassus and Pompey. After conquering Gaul, Caesar got caught in a civil war against Pompey, from which he emerged victorious. In the aftermath, he became dictator for life, thus assuming control of the government of the Republic. Caesar was assassinated in 44 BC, leaving his 19-year-old great-nephew, Octavian (later Augustus) as sole heir.

Lucius **Cassius Dio**: ca. 155–235; Roman historian, author of a Roman history from the founding of Rome to his time. He was a senator, born in Bithynia – incidentally, all his works are written in Greek. He had a high-level political career, serving as governor of Smyrna, Africa and Pannonia.

Flavius **Josephus**: ca. 37–100; Jewish general during the first Jewish-Roman War of sacerdotal and (assumed) royal descent. After surrendering to Vespasian, he becomes the future emperor's slave and interpreter. Subsequently, he acquires citizenship and serves as Vespasian's and Titus'

SHORT BIOGRAPHIES OF THE ANCIENT AUTHORS

advisor. His relation on Jewish history is the most important non-Biblical source on ancient Israel.

Marcus Annaeus **Lucanus**: 39–65; Roman poet, the nephew and pupil of Seneca. While still very young he began to work on *Pharsalia*, an epic poem on the civil war between Caesar and Pompey and became friends with the emperor Nero. Soon enough though the relations deteriorated, Lucanus was involved in a conspiracy and was forced to commit suicide in 65.

Marcus Valerius Martialis (**Martial**): 38/41–102/104; the best known Roman epigrammatist, born in Hispania Tarraconensis. He came to Rome during the last years of Nero's reign and stayed some years into Trajan's reign. He returned to and died in Hispania. He didn't follow a political career and we don't know much of his life outside of literary preoccupation.

Plutarch: ca. 46–119; a Greek historian and philosopher, best known for his biographic *Parallel Lives*. He served as a magistrate in Chaeronea and represented the town in various diplomatic missions. At some point in his live he was granted Roman citizenship. He had good relationships with both Trajan and Hadrian and might have been appointed by the latter *procurator* of Achaea. During his later years he served as a priest in the temple of Apollo at Delphi. Plutarch was a Platonist philosopher and a vegetarian.

Caius **Suetonius** Tranquillus: ca. 69–122; imperial historian, consecrated by the *Lives of the 12 Caesars*. Suetonius comes from a family of knights in Numidia. Educated in Rome, he became a member of the circle of Trajan and later of Hadrian, enjoying the favour of both emperors. In this context, he also has access to valuable sources for the biographies of the Julio-Claudians and Flavians.

Publius Cornelius **Tacitus**: ca. 56–120; probably the best-known Roman historian, author of *Annals* and *Histories*. A member of an equestrian family, he pursued a corresponding career. He married the daughter of Julius Agricola, the general who consolidated Roman rule in Britain. Tacitus is our prime literary source on the Batavians and the Batavian rebellion.

Bibliographical Essay and Bibliography

At the end of this book, we considered that a short presentation of the employed sources might be useful for the reader. Besides the usual bibliographic list, we intend to outline certain aspects for the readers who want to dive deeper into the subject.

The bibliography of the book is built around the major categories of sources. First, we will have the ancient, primary sources; these are literary and epigraphic. The main ancient author describing the Batavians is Tacitus, credible enough due to his connection with Agricola and – at least indirectly – Cerialis. The Latin writers have been quoted in the original, but in the bibliographic list we included an English edition of each of them. These books are nowadays available, annotated and translated, on specialized sites:

- Project Gutenberg: https://www.gutenberg.org/
- Perseus Digital Library: https://www.perseus.tufts.edu/hopper/
- Lacus Curtius: https://penelope.uchicago.edu/Thayer/E/Roman/home.html

The epigraphic sources, stone inscriptions, minor inscriptions (on pots or military equipment) and the Vindolanda tablets can be extracted from epigraphic corpora, which are quoted and referenced in the book and the following list, but they are also available through online repositories:

- Epigraphik Datenbank Heidelberg: https://edh.ub.uni-heidelberg.de/
- Epigraphik Datenbank Clauss/Slaby: http://www.manfredclauss.de/
- Ubi erat Lupa (for photographs): http://lupa.at/
- Roman Inscriptions of Britain: https://romaninscriptionsofbritain.org/

As a dictionary, we used the Oxford Latin Dictionary, which has several print editions and an associated online platform: https://www.oxfordscholarlyeditions.com/page/the-oxford-latin-dictionary.

The next large category is modern historical literature, formed of academic publications, on one side, and excavations and museum reports and catalogues, on the other side. The academic publications are either synthesis (dealing with wider subjects, such as the Roman military, recruitment, Germanic tribes within the Empire, history of certain provinces, etc.), or researches dealing with a very specific topic (articles on face pots, on a certain monument, on a series of names, etc.). From all these we extracted the 'story' of the Batavians. There are many scientific titles on the Batavians, indeed more articles than books, but they deal with very specific matters, written for academics. One of the most noteworthy monographs on Batavian identity, is N. Roymans, *Ethnic Identity*. This is a monograph dealing with the construction of Batavian identity in the Low Rhine area and the tribe's early interactions with the Empire, extremely interesting and exhaustive. A particular feature is the detailed presentation of the Iron Age state of facts and the archaeological realities on which the Batavian materiality came into history. Also seminal are the works of C. van Driel-Murray, who deal specifically with the migration of the troops and the civilians who came along, focusing on Batavians families and their realities. J. Nicolay's *Armed Batavians* is a comprehensive monographs of the arms discovered in the Batavian homeland, their typology and interpretations. We didn't quote in the book, as a general rule, excavation reports, even if they were published as books, because they are extremely technical and irrelevant for the non-specialist public. Rather, we opted for articles on the objects or realities we were describing, or for references in monographs, even if they were not the first publication.

Another title worth mentioning, even if only the electronic format would still be available to buy, is the special number of *Ancient Warfare Magazine* (XV.2/2021), dedicated to the Batavian revolt. The issue is appealing, with rich graphics, but the articles are more or less stand-alone vignettes, without a self-evident red thread. We also have a contribution in the said journal issue, regarding the aftermath of the revolt and the troops' becoming.

There also exists literature, historical fiction, on the Batavian revolt (like A. Riches's *The Centurions* series) or on the troops of Vindolanda (like A. Goldsworthy's *Vindolanda*, part of the *Flavius Ferox* series). Even if these fictions are not extremely numerous or high profile, they can satisfy one's curiosity and transport the reader closer to the Batavians' world.

Following is the list of titles referenced and quoted throughout the book:

Ancient sources

Arrianus, *Ars tactica* (original Greek title: Τέχνη τακτική; for English edition, see: *Flavii Arriani quae exstant omni*. vol. 2. *Scripta minora et fragmenta* (Leipzig, 1968), ed. by A.G. Ross, with additions by G. Wirth).

Caesar, *De bello Alexandrino* (for English edition, see: Caesar, *Alexandrian, African and Spanish wars* (London, Cambridge MA, 1955), Loeb editions, ed. by A.G. Way).

Caesar, *De bello Civili* (for English edition, see: Caesar, *The civil wars* (London, New York, 1914), Loeb editions, ed. by A.G. Peskett).

Caesar, *De bello Gallico* (for English edition, see: Caesar, *The Gallic wars* (London, New York, 1917), Loeb editions, ed. by H.G. Edwards).

Cassius Dio, *Historiae Romanae* (original Greek title: Ῥωμαϊκὴ Ἱστορία; for English edition, see: Cassius Dio, *Roman History* (London, New York, Cambridge MA, 9 volumes, 1914-1927), Loeb editions, ed. by E. Cary).

Josephus, *Jewish War* (original Greek title: Ἱστορία Ἰουδαϊκοῦ πολέμου πρὸς Ῥωμαίους; for English edition, see: *The works of Jopephus. Complete and Unabridged* (Peabody MA, 1987), ed. by W. Whiston).

Lucanus, *Pharsalia* (for English edition, see: Lucan, *The civil war* (London, Cambridge MA, 1928), Loeb editions, ed. by J.D. Duff).

Martial, *Epigrammata* (for English edition, see: Martial, *Epigrams* (London, New York, 1919-1920), Loeb editions, ed. by W C.A. Ker).

Plutarch, *Pyrrhus* (original Greek title: Βίοι Παράλληλοι. Πύρρος; for English edition, see: Plutarch's *Lives*. Vol. IX. *Demetrius and Anthony. Pyrrhus and Caius Marius* (London, Cambridge MA, 1959), Loeb editions, ed. by B. Perrin).

Suetonius, *Caligula* (for English edition, see: Suetonius, *The lives of the twelve Caesars. Caligula* (London, New York, 1913–1914), Loeb editions, ed. by J.C. Rolfe).

Tacitus, *Annales* (for English edition, see: Tacitus, *The Annals* (London, Cambridge MA, 1925–1937), Loeb editions, ed. by J. Jackson).

Tacitus, *De vita et moribus Iulii Agricolae* (for English edition, see: Tacitus, *Agricola. Germania. Dialogus* (London, New York, 1914), Loeb editions, ed. by W. Peterson).

Tacitus, *Germania* (for English edition, see: Tacitus, *Dialogus. Germania. Agricola* (London, New York, 1914), Loeb editions, ed. by W. Peterson).

Tacitus, *Historiae* for English edition, see: Tacitus, *The Histories* (London, Cambridge MA, 1925-1937), Loeb editions, ed. by C. H. Moore).

Collections of works and encyclopaedias

AE: *L'Année Epigraphique*, Paris, 1888–.
CIL: *Corpus Inscriptionum Latinarum*, Berlin, 1893–.
Encyclopædia Britannica, vol. 5 (11th ed.) (Cambridge: Cambridge University Press, 1910–1911); online: https://www.britannica.com/ .

Tabulae Vindolandenses: Vindolanda: The Latin writing tablets, Britannia Monograph Series, 4 volumes, 1983–2019.

References

G. Alföldy, *Die Hilfstruppen der römischen Provinz Germania Inferior* (Düsseldorf: Rheinland Verlag, 1968).

A. Birley, 'The names of the Batavians and Tungrians', in T. Grünewald (ed.), *Germania inferior. Besiedllung, Gesellschaft und Wirtschaft an der Grenze der römisch-germanischen Welt*, RGA Ergänzungsband 28 (Berlin, New York: de Gruyter, 2001).

A. Bowman, 'Outposts of empire: Vindolanda, Egypt and the empire of Rome', *Journal of Roman Archaeology* 19, 2006.

G. Bounegru, R. Varga, 'Two face pots from the vicus of Războieni-Cetate (Alba County)', in S. Nemeti, E. Beu-Dachin, I. Nemeti, D. Dana (eds.), *The Roman provinces. Mechanisms of integration* (Cluj-Napoca: Mega Publishing House, 2020).

M.D. Carroll, 'Civic ideology and its subversion: Rembrandt's "Oath of Claudius Civilis"', *Art History*, 9, 1986.

N. Cesarik, 'The inscription of a Batavian horseman from the Archaeological Museum Zadar', *Zeitschrift für Papyrologie und Epigraphik*, 199, 2016.

I. Clegg, 'Martial rape and the Batavian revolt. Shameful behaviour', *Ancient warfare*, XV/2, 2022.

P. Cosme, 'L'impact de la guerre civile de 68-70 sur le recrutement des auxiliaires', *HIMA*, 6, 2017.

D.B. Cuff, 'The King of the Batavians: Remarks on Tab Vindol. III, 628', *Britannia*, 42, 2011.

B. van Daele,'The military fabricae in Germania Inferior from Augustus to A.D. 260/270', *JRMES*, 10, 1999.

M. Dahm, 'The end of the Batavian revolt. Mopping up', *Ancient warfare*, XV/2, 2022.

T. Derks, 'Ethnic identity in the Roman frontier. The epigraphy of Batavi and other Lower Rhine tribes', in T. Derks, N. Roymans (eds.), *Ethnic Constructs in Antiquity. The role of power and tradition* (Amsterdam: Amsterdam University Press, 2009).

T. Derks, H. Teitler, 'Batavi in the Roman Army of the Principate', *BJB*, 218, 2018.

E. Dickey, *Latin forms of Address: from Plautus to Apuleius* (Oxford: Oxford University Press, 2002).

C. van Driel-Murray, 'Ethnic Soldiers: The Experience of the Lower Rhine Tribes', in T. Grunewald, S. Seibel (eds.), *Kontinuitat und Diskontinuitat* (Berlin: de Gruyter, 2003).

W. Eck, 'Militärisches und ziviles Alltagsleben am Hadrianswall', *JRA* 18, 2002.

G. Elmer, 'Die Münzprägung der gallischen Kaiser von Postumus bis Tetricus in Köln, Trier und Mailand', *BJB*, 146, 1941.

H. Enckevort, J. Thijssen (eds.), *In de schaduw van het Noorderlicht. De Gallo-Romeinse tempel van Elst-Westeraam* (Nijmegen: Bureau Archeologie Gemeente, 2005).

J. Garbsch, *Römische Paraderüstungen* (München: Beck's, 1978), p. 100.

C. Gazdac, G. Bounegru, R. Varga, 'Paying and saving in Gold in The Roman Army. The Aureus of Vespasian from Războieni-Cetate and the evidence of Gold Coins in Roman Dacia (Romania)', *Journal of Ancient History and Archaeology*, 7/2, 2020, pp. 94–102.

A. Goldsworthy, *The complete Roman army* (London: Thames & Hudson, 2003), pp. 57–58.

A. Goldsworthy, 'Send beer!' Life on the Roman frontier revealed by soldiers' private letters', National Geographic (online, published June 28, 2023).

J.K. Haalebos, 'Traian und die Hilfstruppen am Niederrhein. Ein Militiirdiplom des Jahren 98 n. Chr. aus Elst in der Overbetuwe (Niederlande)', *Saalburg Jahrbuch*, 50, 2000.

D. Habermehl *et. al.*, 'Investigating migration and mobility in the Early Roman frontier. The case of the Batavi in the Dutch Rhine Delta (ca. 50–30 BC–AD 40)', *Germania*, 100, 2022.

E.O.G. Haitsma Mulier, 'Grotius, Hooft and the writing of Dutch history in the Dutch Republic', in A.C. Duke, C.A. Tamse (eds.), *Clio`s mirror. Historiography in Britain and The Netherlands* (Zutphen: De Walburg Pers, 1985).

M.W.C. Hassall, 'Batavians and the Roman Conquest of Britain', *Britannia* 1, 1970.

S. Heeren, 'The material culture of small rural settlements in the Batavian area: a case study on discrepant experience, Creolisation, Romanisation or Globalisation?', in H. Platts *et al.* (eds.), *TRAC 2013: Proceedings of the Twenty-Third Annual Theoretical Roman Archaeology Conference, King's College, London 2013* (Oxford: Oxbow Books, 2014).

P. van der Heijden, A. Koster, *Romeinse helmen in Nederland* (Leiden: Hazenberg Archeologie, 2017)

T. Ivleva, 'British emigrants in the Roman Empire: complexities and symbols of ethnic identities', in D. Mladenovic, B. Russel, *Trac 2010* (Oxford: Oxbow Books, 2011).

L.I. Kooistra, *Borderland Farming. Possibilities and limitations of farming in the Roman period and early Middle Ages between Rhine and Meuse* (Assen/Amersfoort: Van Gorcum/Rijksdienst voor Oudheidkundig Bodemonderzoek, 1996).

B. Lorincz, *Die romischen Hilfstruppen in Pannonien wiihrend der Prinzipatszeit*. Teil I: *Die lnschriften* (Wien: Phoibos, 2001).

K. Narloch, 'The cold face of battle – some remarks on the function of roman helmets with face masks', *Archäologisches Korrespondenzblatt*, 42, 2002.

S. Nemeti, R. Varga, D. Deac, 'A vignette from Dacia under Philippus Arabs: revisiting the altars of Marcus Publicianus Rhenus', *Chiron,* 2024, pp. 429-448.

J. Nicolay, *Armed Batavians. Use and significance of weaponry and horse gear from non-military contexts in the Rhine Delta (50 BC to AD 450)* (Amsterdam: Amsterdam University Press, 2007).

J. Oldenstein, 'Zur Buntmetallverarbeitung in den Kastellen am obergermanischen und rätischen Limes', *Bulletin des Musees Royaux d'art et d'histoire*, 6, 1974.

S. Rocca, *The army of Herod the Great* (Oxford: Osprey Publishing, 2009).

J.A. van Rossum, 'The End of the Batavian Auxiliaries as "National" Units', in L. de Light (ed.), *Roman rule and civic life: local and regional perspectives. Proceedings of the Fourth Workshop of the International Network "Impact of Empire (Roman Empire, c. 200 B.C. – A. D. 476)", Leiden, June 25–28, 2003* (Amsterdam: Brill, 2004).

N. Roymans, *Ethnic identity and imperial power. The Batavians in the early Roman Empire* (Amsterdam: Amsterdam University Press, 2004).

A. Rubel, C. Mischka, 'Of horses and men – Garrisoning the empire: stable-barracks on a grand scale in the auxiliary fort of the ala I Batavorum milliaria at Războieni-Cetate (Alba Iulia County, Romania) and the spatial planning of Roman forts', *Journal of Roman Archaeology*, 36, 2023.

C. Rummel, *The fleets on the northern frontier of the Roman Empire from 1st to 3rd century* (PhD thesis: University of Nottingham, 2008).

H.D.J. Van Schevichaven, *Epigraphie der Bataafsche krijgslieden in de Romeinsche legers, gevolgd van een lijst van alle geregelde hulptroepen tijdens het Keizerrijk* (Leiden: Bij A. E. Sijthoff, 1881).

I. Schöffer, 'The Batavian myth during the sixteenth and seventeenth centuries, in J.S. Bromley, E.H. Kossmann (eds.), *Britain and the Netherlands V. Some political mythologies. Papers delivered to the fifth Anglo-Dutch Historical Conference* (The Hague: Nijhoff, 1975).

J. Slofstra, 'Batavians and Romans on the Lower Rhine', *Archaeological Dialogues*, 9, 2002.

C.S. Sommer, '"Where did they put the horses?": Überlegungen zu Aufbau und Stärkerömischer Auxiliartruppen und deren Unterbringung in den in den Kastellen', in: W. Czysz *et al.* (eds.), *Provinzialrömische Forschungen. Festschrift für Günter Ulbert zum 65. Geburtstag* (Espelkamp: Verlag M. Leidorf, 1995).

J. Spaul, *Cohors. The evidence for and a short history of the auxiliary infantry units of the Imperial Roman Army*, BAR International Series 841 (Oxford: Archaeopress, 2000).

M.P. Speidel, *Riding for Caesar* (London, New York: Routledge, 1994).

M P. Speidel, *Ancient Germanic warriors* (London, New York: Routledge, 2004).

B.H. Stolte, 'Die religiösen Verhältnisse in Niedergermanien', in W. Haase (ed.), Aufstieg und Niedergang der römischen Welt, Bd. II 18, 1 Religion (Heidentum: Die religiösen Verhältnisse in den Provinzen) (Berlin, New York 1986).

K. Strobel, 'Anmerkungen zur Geschichte der Bataverkohorten in der hohen Kaiserzeit', *ZPE*, 70, 1987.

Tg., 'Római sisak Székely-Kocsárdról', Archaeologiai Értesítő, 1888, pp. 184–185.

R. Varga, A. Rubel, G. Bounegru, 'Pottery vessels with *graffiti* discovered in the fort of *ala I Batavorum* in Dacia', *Electrum*, 2024, pp. 127-141.

I. Vossen, 'The possibilities and limitations of demographic calculations in the Batavian area', in in T. Grunewald, S. Seibel (eds.), *Kontinuitat und Diskontinuitat* (Berlin: de Gruyter, 2003), pp. 414–435.

I. Vossen, M. Groot, 'Barley and horses: surplus and demand in the *civitas Batavorum*', in M. Driessen *et al.*(eds.), *TRAC 2008*, (Oxford: Oxbow Books, 2009)

Paul Weiss, 'Neue Diplome für Soldaten der Exercitus Dacicus', *ZPE*, 141, 2002.

W.J.H. Willems, 'Romans and Batavians. A regional study in the Dutch Eastern River Area', *BROB*, 34, 1984.

W.J.H. Willems, *Romans and Batavians. A regional study in the Dutch Eastern Area* (PhD thesis: University of Amsterdam, 1986).

W.J.H. Willems, H. van Enckevort, *Vlpia Noviomagus. Roman Nijmegen. The Batavian capital at the imperial frontier*, JRA Supplementary series, 73, 2009.

M.J.M. Zandstra, *Miles away from home. Material culture as a guide to the composition and deployment of the Roman army in the Lower Rhine area during the 1st century AD* (Nijmegen: Radbound Universiteit, 2019)

M. Zerjadtke, 'Germanic warriors and amphibious warfare. No barrier to battle', *Ancient warfare*, XV/2, 2022.

About the author

Rada Varga is a researcher at Cluj-Napoca University, with a PhD in Ancient History. She specialises in social history, material culture and the history of the 'common people' (non-elites) of the Roman Empire. The platform she coordinates, Romans1by1, won the DH Award 2019 for the best DH dataset. As an archaeologist, she excavates at the site where the ala I Batavorum was stationed for more than 100 years in Dacia. She is the author of several scientific books and articles published by Routledge, Archaeopress, Harrassowitz, Brill. In addition to her academic work, she has been involved in the popularisation of history, writing for Ancient Warfare and the best-known Romanian history popularisation magazine, Historia (her article on the Batavians was the cover article and the issue was the best-selling of 2021).

About the artist

Giorgio Albertini was born in 1968 in Milan where he still lives. After studying Medieval History at the University of Milan, he become involved in archaeology and has been involved in several excavations for European institutions. He was responsible for the graphic depiction of archaeological sites and finds. He also works as a historical and scientific illustrator for many institutions, museums, and magazines such as *National Geographic Magazine, BBC History,* and *Medieval Warfare*. He has always been interested in military history and is one of the founders of *Focus Wars* magazine.

Titles in the From Alexander to Adrianople series:

No 1   *The Army of Alexander the Great* by Richard Taylor (ISBN 978-1-804517-70-3)

No 2   *Leuktra 371 BCE: Sparta's Twilight* by Nic Fields (ISBN 978-1-804517-69-7)

No 3   *Fortissimi and Validissimi: The Batavian Auxiliaries of the Roman Army* by Rada Varga (ISBN 978-1-804518-26-7)